AN IOWA HAP

HARTLEY A. "HAP" WESTBROOK

A biography of a decorated bomber pilot during World War II, prisoner of war, member of the Iowa Aviation Hall of Fame and an airport operator for over fifty years.

by Norman Rudi

McMillen Publishing
A Sigler Company
515-232-6997
413 Northwestern, P.O. Box 887
Ames, Iowa 50010-0887

Library of Congress Control Number 2001092394
ISBN Number 1-888223-25-1

An Iowa Pilot Named Hap

DEDICATION

This book is dedicated to the thousands of young men and women who served in World War II, who sacrificed in untold ways to preserve our freedom,

And

To the Prisoner of War survivors who helped build a nation unequaled in history,

And

To Ann who can read me like a book.

An Iowa Pilot Named Hap

INTRODUCTION

On June 24th, 2000, Hartley Westbrook was inducted into the Iowa Aviation Hall of Fame at a ceremony in Greenfield, Iowa. Recognition for a lifetime of service, to not only the Iowa Aviation Industry but aviation in general, was appropriate and well deserved. Westbrook's career as a WW II bomber pilot, prisoner of war, ranking pilot in the Iowa National Guard, and forty years of fixed base operation is without peer.

Tom Brokow's book, *The Greatest Generation*, called attention to the participation and contribution of men and women who tested human endurance, and survived to contribute significantly to our world today. The renewed interest in the myriad of individual contributions and experiences has fostered great interest in individual stories.

When Westbrook gave a presentation to the local Rotary Club after being recognized for his contribution to Iowa Aviation, it was apparent there was more to his story than a twenty-minute presentation. After several sessions with Westbrook, his story evolved into a number of interesting experiences, many of which are included in this book. The history of the Eighth Air Force is well documented in books, movies and personal accounts. Beyond the glory is a story of personal sacrifice, deprivation, fortitude, and struggle for survival of human will.

After WW II, prisoners of war were reluctant to reveal their personal experiences to the general public. Post-military journals provided a venue for interacting with friends and acquaintances from that period in their life. These were not widely distributed.

In this effort Hartley Westbrook chose to emphasize conditions surrounding being a prisoner of war. For several years, we watched the TV show "Hogan's Heros" and associated the experience as a fun, devil-may-care experience. In remembering times gone by we tend to remember the good times and put bad experiences in a very private compartment.

Perhaps a review of coping with extraordinary circumstances will re-introduce a sense of reality during difficult times in an accomplished life.

Hartley "Hap" Westbrook holding a model of a B-24 Liberator bomber which is on display in his office.

TABLE OF CONTENTS

An Iowa Pilot Named Hap

CHAPTER ONE
DESCENT

Through the haze and clouds, one could barely make out the landfall of the north German peninsula. The targets today were the submarine bases in Kiel, Germany, a major port for the submarine wolfpacks inflicting untold damage to the Allied shipping in the North Atlantic. The B-24 Liberator labored under its load of six thousand pounds of incendiary bombs, and waist gunners readied their fifty caliber machine guns for the Messerschmitt 109s and Focke-Wulf 190s that would soon be dropping out of nowhere.

A sudden explosion in the tail section perforated the fuselage with shrapnel, instantly killing the tail gunner and the two waist gunners. Two FW 190s swung into position and raked the plane with machine-gun fire right to left. Engines one and two blew out, engine three started missing and engine four trailed flames. The Liberator started to descend in a wide spiral and Lieutenant Westbrook opened the bomb bay doors and jettisoned the incendiaries. While doing this he shouted orders for the remaining crew to leave the ship. The co-pilot dropped through the bomb bay doors, and the navigator and bombardier cranked down the nose wheel, their only way out. The FW-190s made another pass, with bullets shattering the instrument panel. A bullet penetrated Westbrook's right shoulder, and shrapnel tore through his flying suit, chewing up his right knee and calf. Westbrook fought the controls to guide the turning plane without success; then, sensing the futility, dropped down to the flight deck 30" below.

Tufts of fabric expanded out of the English parachute where it had been raked by shrapnel, but he managed to pull on the harness, and twist lock the safety. He saw a member of the crew sitting on the edge of the bomb bay, dangling his feet, afraid to jump. He grabbed a fuselage rib and with his bleeding leg, placed it in the back of the young man and pushed him out the bomb bay door.

Approaching landfall at 19,000 feet, the plane had been in a steady decline since he had turned out to sea. In the few minutes since the attack had occurred, the plane had traveled fifteen to twenty miles into the Baltic Sea. Amid the smell of hot oil, gasoline and cordite, Westbrook took one last look around, then tumbled out of the bomb bay doors.

His parachute blossomed, his ears popped, and the oxygen container strapped to his leg flew away, jerking out his mouthpiece and two and one-half of Westbrook's front teeth. Through the pain, he sensed that it was incredibly quiet. He looked up at the canopy, and found it polka dotted with torn openings and tufts of fabric trailing upward. He was oscillating wildly in the strong wind when he heard a loud explosion and saw the Liberator disintegrate before his eyes.

In Westbrook's words, "After leaving the aircraft, I came to realize that I was out in the world by myself. The first thing I noticed was the intense silence, lack of engine noise, and being completely out of the aircraft with no support but a parachute. Then and only then, did I come to the reality that I was alone now, and to survive, it was up to me. Now was the time to use the survival emergency skills I had been schooled and briefed on previously.

"I could see water for miles and no sign of a life raft or boat, and no visible land. It was a hopeless situation but I didn't want to give up. Then I realized I couldn't survive in the icy water and worried that Mother and Jane would not know where I was. I would have liked to inform my family of what had happened and how I died. The pendulum action lifted me sideways and dropped me into the icy water like a body slam. The cold North Sea water burned my open wounds, and the cold water had me gasping for breath.

"I can remember vividly finding that my sheepskin-lined boots made good anchors, and gasping for breath, diving down and unzipping the boots and discarding them. I fought the water for a time until my body felt numb and I gasped for breath in the cold, choppy sea. I finally relaxed, totally exhausted and drifted into unconsciousness. Evidently, I must have floated face up because I was found several hours later. How anyone found me in all that rough water is a miracle."

CHAPTER TWO
LETTS, IOWA

The two-bottomed cultivator scuffed through the sandy loam turning weeds as Hartley Westbrook walked alongside through the rows of corn. It was nearly the summer solstice, and the warm June morning increased the possibility of the corn being "knee high by the fourth of July." The heat of July would cause the corn to grow rapidly, but first it had to be plowed, then crossed through the drilled hills of corn aligned with military precision. Pet and Bonnie, Hartley's young mares, moved quickly at his insistence. After this field was crossed, there were sixty acres at Hariff's and forty acres at Lloyd Rouch's farm to complete before the corn was too tall to plow and laid aside.

Westbrook was lucky. Living on a farm a couple of miles from Letts, Iowa, in the river flatland only twenty or so miles from the great Mississippi river, meant the Westbrook family was spared many of the problems of the depression. He and his five brothers and two sisters had plenty to do, contributing to the family's subsistence. Although there was little cash flow, there was plenty to eat. There were twenty cows to produce milk, cream and butter. There were pigs for butchering, chickens and ducks. Each one of the boys had a team of horses, and after tilling their own land, could hire out for fifty cents per day plus horse feed. Dad and Mother assigned everyone a list of duties, and each child performed their tasks without question. There was a job to do and you did it.

Tilling, haying, threshing and any additional job was needed for a few pennies to salt away. Hartley had graduated from Grandview High School a year earlier in 1937, and it would take two full summers to acquire the funds to attend Teachers College. Since Dad was paying for the education of two of the older children, Hartley would be responsible for paying for his own education. He would have to work while in college and every summer. As long as Pet and Bonnie were taken care of by his brothers while he was away, he could continue to hire out during summer. After all Pet and Bonnie had carried him through high school. He had signed on to drive a school hack picking up fifteen or twenty students on the way to school. For three years that money found its way to the bank and helped establish the dream.

The Westbrook children attended a one-room school for the first eight years of schooling. The township school was only a half-mile from the Westbrook home and rigidly followed the Iowa law that "each school shall have one well, two outhouses and twelve trees." That Iowa law was finally modified by the legislature in 1952 when school consolidations made one-room schools obsolete. Rural teachers used the older students to assist the younger students, and June Harter, the teacher at Forresthill Township School used it to good advantage. It reinforced the learning process and let the students feel comfortable learning at their own speed from their peers. For Hartley, it developed skills he would use the rest of his life.

At the end of the row of corn, the horses wheeled about and Hartley stopped the team for a breather; perhaps two more passes before having lunch, which was packed in a one-gallon honey pail stored in the tall grass in the far fencerow. The air was fresh, and meadowlarks sang from the fence posts. In two more months, Westbrook would be sitting in a classroom, with other new students. He could sleep past five-thirty in the morning, and would not have morning and evening chores. He could study by electric light, play sports, and meet girls.

Bonnie whinnied and pawed the ground. It was time to move on, and suddenly lunch sounded good. Two more passes, then lunch.

This was a good farm. Benjamin Harrison Westbrook felt that when he first put foot on it. There was no need to move further west. With his wife, Mabel, they improved the homestead and raised eight children. They were of English, Scottish, German and Dutch origins, and incorporated the work ethic and survival instincts of their forebearers. They started their family when Jenatta was born in 1914. Benjamin Harrison Jr. joined the family in 1916 and Fredrick in 1917. Hartley came into the world on January 29, 1919, followed by Robert in 1921, Jessie Lee in 1924, Donald Ralph in 1927 and finally Richard, born in 1929. It was a full farmhouse, but from the start each family member was given a role and responsibility. There were no options. You did your part.

Mabel (Wagner) Westbrook and Benjamin A Westbrook, Hartley's parents, were successful farming several hundred acres outside Letts, IA. They raised eight children and imbued them with an appreciation for education and a solid work ethic.

With five young men, each with their own team of horses, the crops were planted, tilled and harvested. This gave father Benjamin the opportunity to raise additional crops to supplement family income. There was twenty-five acres set aside for growing cucumbers, tomatoes and cabbage plants. In addition after the corn was laid by, pumpkin seeds were planted among the corn, which matured after the corn was picked. These crops could be sold at the Heintz canning factory in Muscatine, for which Ben received real dollars. This income provided school clothes for the children and other necessities during the depression years.

For a family of ten, the farm was self-sustaining. There were fifteen to twenty milk cows that provided milk. The family separated the milk and cream and churned their own butter. There were fifty to one hundred cattle to be fed and marketed. A few pigs were raised for home processing. Chickens and ducks roamed the farmstead. They kept twenty head of horses for use around the farm. A large garden provided the vegetables for canning to provide for the long winter months. A small orchard with whitney and winesap apple trees provided for apple pies. At harvest time the winesaps were individually wrapped in newspapers and stored in a wooden barrel in the basement, to be enjoyed with popcorn on long winter nights.

The depression year of 1934 was a low point for the Westbrook family. Grain crops had not been good and grain prices were low. At Christmas time the children went to the nearby woods and cut an oak branch to be used as a Christmas tree. The boys made popcorn and string garlands, and the sisters made bows from scrap pieces of fabric. Each child was permitted one candleholder and candle to mount on the extreme branches of the tree. Two buckets of water were on standby in case one of the eight candles created a problem. The sparse tree reflected on the sparse gifts to be received that year. Reflecting on past Christmas celebrations, Hartley remembers it as being one of the most memorable.

The windmill and elevated water tank provided water to the house. The cistern that collected rainwater from the house eaves was used for laundry. The Westbrook family did not enjoy indoor plumbing until the year Hartley left for college, 1938, and REA electric line did not arrive until 1940.

The Westbrook farm adjoined timberland leading to the river. Several sawmills harvested timber in the area, and it was reported that sawmill operators also serviced several moonshine liquor stills. The area became locally known as "Whiskey Hollow Hill," a name not favored by Benjamin Sr. because of his Methodist upbringing.

The family butchered their own animals and processed them at home. The boys ground meat cuttings into sausage and stuffed it in animal casings. One day while preparing sausage, the boys were enjoying a break by eating popcorn delivered by the sisters. When they again started stuffing the casings, Hartley took a handful of "old maids" and slipped them into the sausage. The sausage was smoked and stored. The next summer, father Ben sat down to a delicious breakfast of fried eggs, toast, hash browns and homemade sausage. His first bite encountered an unpopped kernel, which broke his false teeth. He never said a word, but he knew which free spirit had caused the "old maids" to be added to the sausage.

An Iowa Pilot Named Hap

Life on the farm was dictated by the intense daily effort to meet the demands of the animals, the chores, and the growing and harvesting seasons. There was no letup from the daily routine, and the family obligingly performed their respective responsibilities. Each family member contributed to the total effort and was rewarded by being a part of a caring, self-sufficient family life. A solid Methodist faith and strong Republican views prepared the family members for a life of service.

Janetta married an engineer and lived in Des Moines. Benjamin Jr. became a farmer, continuing in his father's footsteps. Fredrick became a minister in the Methodist faith. Hartley had a career in aviation. Robert became an engineer, flew B-24s and completed fifty missions in WW II, while Hartley was a POW. Jessie Lee became a schoolteacher. Donald Ralph became a rancher in California. And Richard, the youngest, became a missionary and an ordained minister. The routine of responsibility in their early years led to serving their fellow man and contributing to the social fabric we call America.

Pet and Bonnie knew it was time for a break, and when they reached the fencerow refused to turn. Hartley unhitched them, and looped the harness over barbed wire. They whinnied and nibbled at grass along the fencerow, while he wiped the sweat from under their harnesses with an old shirt. Horses, like people, respond to special attention when they have been put to test. He then walked down the fencerow where he uncovered his lunch pail and canvas water bag from the tall grass and sat down, leaning against the wooden fence post. A long drink of the warm water took the grit out of his mouth and a quick squirt on the face removed the morning's dust.

Unwrapping the meatloaf sandwich, he again contemplated attending college. The fifty cents per day for driving the school hack had netted him almost three hundred dollars for three years. Driving the school hack was a chore. In addition to managing fifteen to twenty rambunctious children, he also had to clean the bus each week, take care of the horses, and still perform in the classroom. He had to have a stack of wood for the small stove which sat behind the driver's cab. In cold weather with the stove going full blast, the cab over heated, and the hack distributed heat unevenly throughout the rest of the bus. Some days he would move students around so they could have their share of warmth. They were quick to respond in their heavy corduroy sheepskins and hand-knitted mittens.

Hartley's good disposition and cheerfulness were known and appreciated by the children, and they hopped to whenever he suggested a change in their boisterous activity. When he gave a command, they immediately complied, for as long as school children can.

Early spring, when the frost went out of the ground, was always the worst time to drive a school hack. The mud roads had no bottom, and Pet and Bonnie had a difficult time gaining footing. The hack had to be cleaned every night, both inside and out, after the evening chores were done. The money he made was added to the college fund.

Hartley reviewed the tasks to be accomplished the rest of the summer, because in two months Hartley would begin a new, exciting activity.

A lone biplane droned overhead through the scattered puff clouds, and was ignored by the young man considering the summer ahead. As he went over the numbers in his mind, by August he would have enough money in the bank to start Teachers College this fall. There was no time to consider the biplane, where it was going or what it was up to. There was work to be done. There had to be money in the bank in order to have a career in coaching.

CHAPTER THREE
TEACHERS COLLEGE

The occupants of the four-door Dodge were suddenly silent. Saying goodbyes at the house was almost raucous, with Hartley's brothers teasing him about young girls he was about to encounter. Since father was helping two children to attend college, Hartley would have to pay his own way. Ben Sr. reminded Hartley to write his mother whenever possible. Now Ben Jr. and Fredrick were quiet. They would miss their younger brother, particularly during threshing season. They would miss his good humor and his happy-go-lucky attitude, as well as the extra pair of hands.

They stopped at the intersection of Highway 92, and Hartley

Happy-go-lucky "Happy" Westbrook proudly wearing his "Class of 42" sweater at Iowa State Teachers College.

retrieved his two heavy suitcases from the rear seat. He was wearing his high school basketball letter sweater, since no driver could resist giving a lift to a young college student. Hitching a ride was commonplace, and usually the time spent traveling was less than taking the bus. He shook hands with his brothers, gave his father an extended hug, picked up his suitcases and walked to the edge of the highway. It was not without some apprehension that he raised his arm, made a fist and motioned with his thumb. The second car stopped and gave him a ride twenty miles to Highway 218, where he repeated the action and started riding north to Cedar Falls and Teachers College.

The first year at Iowa State Teachers College, Hartley lived in the college dormitory. He managed to get a board job at a local restaurant, where for three hours a day, he dutifully did every menial task assigned. Because of his cheerful disposition and happy-go-lucky attitude, the meliorist was given the nickname Happy. Because of the traffic and visibility working in the restaurant, Happy became a permanent moniker.

The year was 1939, and although there was turmoil abroad, central United States was finally experiencing a release from the mindset of the depression. The transition from a year-and-a-half of farming to resuming study skills was not without some trying moments for Happy. His solidly ingrained work habits prevailed and even with working several hours a day at the restaurant, Happy survived his first year with good grades. His attitude and work habits were noticed by acquaintances and he was asked to join the Sigma Alpha Epsilon fraternity. The prospect of living off campus with perhaps a bit more freedom of expression appealed to Happy, and he became a member. Most of his new fraternity brothers were from the same rural background, and their economic status, like Happy's, was stretched to the limit.

After a summer on the farm, Happy returned to Teachers College for his sophomore year, and lived in the fraternity house. He found work in another restaurant, as well as a part-time job in the greenhouse plucking dead leaves and doing general cleanup.

That fall the students at Teachers College were entranced with a new popular song ascribed to Swedish origin, but actually gibberish, that had everyone singing. Staying current with popular songs was a major pastime, but this song was particularly catchy. It went, "Hut Sut Rawlson on the rillerah and a brawla brawla soo-et. The Rawlson is a Swedish town, and the rillerah is a stream. The brawla is a boy and girl, and the hut sut is their dream." It was so popular that it topped the 1936 song "The Music Goes Round and Round," and the 1939 song "Three Little Fishies." The young students, far from the troubles in Europe, were living their dream and lustily contributed to the song's popularity.

In October, a young lady acquaintance, Jane Bowers, asked Happy to double date with her roommate, Angie, at a college party. The evening and the party were going quite well when Jane and Happy found a corner of the living room to have a quiet conversation. They spent a half hour discussing whatever college students

Jane Bowers attended Bayard High School and looked forward to becoming a school teacher like her mother.

discuss at parties and found several mutual interests. After a most friendly discussion Happy suggested he take Jane back to the dorm. Jane accepted the invitation and they left the party together leaving their dates to fend for themselves. Angie was so distraught that Jane had left with Happy, she packed her bags the next day, left school and went home.

After that evening, Jane and Happy dated occasionally, but each had many friends and enjoyed their college life. Happy found a good buy in a four-door Model A Ford, and decided he could help pay for it by offering rides to students headed home for the holidays for one dollar. It proved to be a good investment because upon returning home, Dad would fill the car with gas, plus give him some spending money. The added bonus was most of the riders were girls, since they could not hitchhike like the boys. Thanksgiving, Christmas, quarter break and Easter were special breaks in many ways.

Happy continued to work in the restaurant and was visited one day by Jane. Happy continued to work while openly flirting with the attractive co-ed. While slicing an onion, the knife slipped, and caused a large gash across his thumb, which required several stitches, and lots of attention from Jane. The scar from that incident is still apparent fifty years later, and a reminder of their involvement. Happy started showing apt attention to the young lady, and they started seeing each other more frequently.

Jane Bowers was raised on a farm in Guthrie County, Iowa. Although the family farm was only two miles from Coon Rapids, it was in the Bayard School District, and Jane and her younger sister Ethel, named after her mother, traveled the six miles to attend school there all twelve years. The family farm was a grain farm, but contained all the elements necessary to be self-sustaining during the difficult times. The farm had preserved ten acres of virgin prairie used as pasture for their horses. Jane's mother practiced the rural frugality, making all of the girls' dresses and coats. Dresses made from patterned feed sacks were commonplace, but an occasional trip to the fabric shop for new patterns and ribbons was a special event. The sisters did not expect much and always appreciated and took care of the things they did receive.

Jane's mother, Ethel, was a schoolteacher in Pennsylvania, which probably contributed to the family's interest and continuation in that service. Ethel accompanied her father to Bayard, Iowa, to visit a brother, where she met a young farmer, Ed Bowers. A romance blossomed, and within a year they were married.

One of Jane's duties was to carry several pails of water each day from the pump house to the kitchen for use in the house. She had additional farm chores, and her mother made certain she did her share of house cleaning. Growing up on the farm meant playing in the haymow in winter, helping can vegetables in the summer and an occasional Saturday night trip to town to sell eggs and cream, buy groceries and catch up on the latest news around town. Jane's father was very strict with the girls and watched the Saturday excursions very carefully.

Jane and Ethel had a coal black Shetland pony that was their pride. They would often ride "Blackie" a half-mile to the neighbor's farm to play with children their age. The neighbors also had a Shetland pony, which made riding trips around the hills great fun. Farms were not yet mechanized and horses were a part of the family. Blackie lived to be twenty-seven years old, and was kept on the farm long after the girls had left for college.

One of the sisters' treasured memories was visiting an uncle's farm that contained an excellent sledding hill. On a cold winter's night under a full moon, Jane, sister Ethel, and the neighbors' children, would fly down the hill on their steel runner sleds. After several hours they would warm up with hot chocolate, then bundle up with warm, dry scarves and mittens and crawl into the bobsled for a trip home under the full moon. It was a memory that most

Iowa farm children would share.

The winter of 1935-36 was one of the most severe in Iowa, and snowdrifts and cold temperatures isolated farmsteads and discouraged travel. The temperature dropped to below zero and remained there for twenty days. The temperature, plus an inordinate sequence of storms that created drifts eight to ten feet high, brought normal winter activity to a halt. Farmers feared for their livestock, and their own well being. Some schools closed for several weeks because the school inside temperature could not be raised above fifty degrees. Drifts covered fence lines and obliterated the definition of roadways. The Bayard superintendent kept the school open for townspeople who could attend. Farm students who had schoolbooks tried to keep up with assigned lessons. The Bowers hitched a pair of horses to a box bobsled, wrapped the children in blankets and traveled cross-country to deliver the children of several families to school, and the return trip included groceries needed to provide food for the families.

The Bowers were Methodists and attended church regularly when the condition of the roads and the weather permitted. Church socials were always a high point, and the church dinners introduced special foods and treats, rarely seen at home.

Jane graduated from Bayard High School in 1936, and started Teachers College that fall. Her interest in elementary education and the anticipation of security of employment influenced her decision. The Teachers College had a high ratio of girls to boys because the profession of teaching was one of the acceptable activities for young ladies. The school offered excellent preparation for elementary and secondary education and was nationally recognized. Jane's ability to learn came naturally, and she did not have to study as hard as her younger sister. Ethel graduated in 1938 and went to Teachers College for a year, then attended Drake in Des Moines, also getting her degree in elementary education. Ethel married a farmer, Ed Honnold, and moved to the farm but continued to teach.

When Ed Bowers heard that Happy was taking flying lessons, he expressed to Jane in his protective way, "Jane, I hope you will never go up in an airplane." Jane giggled and said, "Dad, you are too late. I have been up several times."

Fem's Fancy was the girl-ask-boy college fall dance, featuring a big band that passed through the Waterloo-Cedar Falls area on a regular basis. Waterloo/Cedar Falls was on the route from Chicago to Omaha, where the big bands would play weekends, but play for dances in small towns on Tuesday, Wednesday, Thursday and Friday. It exposed small town Iowa to most of the major bands of that period. The College would arrange for a big dance, usually one per quarter, and it was always a special occasion. Jane had asked Happy as her date, since this was a special ballroom dance.

Happy had been working the evening meal at the restaurant, and picked up Jane, asking her to wait in the fraternity living room while he showered and changed clothes. Jane patiently waited on a couch in the living room, when suddenly two young men, "naked as jaybirds" dashed down the stairs, snapping wet towels at each other. They energetically attacked each other, unaware of the young lady on the couch. Jane covered her eyes with her hands, hoping not to be hit with a wild shot. After several minutes, realizing they were being observed, the fraternity brothers dashed upstairs, much more red from embarrassment than towel damage. Jane always claimed that she did not recognize either of the fraternity men.

In the spring of 1939, Happy became interested in flying. He and several young men signed up for Citizens Pilot Training to take flying lessons. The lessons cost fifty dollars, and Happy did not have the money in hand at that time. He contacted his maternal Grandmother Wagner for a loan. She was quite fond of Happy and forwarded the money, although in those days flying was not an upstanding pursuit since it was considered the choice of ''ne'er-do-wells and unstable young men" searching for adventure. Westbrook then went to the Waterloo Airport and signed up for lessons with Jon and Bite Livingston, flying instructors at the airport.

Both Bite and Jon Livingston had learned to fly in Dayton, Ohio, in the 1920s. Their official pilot licenses were signed by Orville Wright.

Several years later Jon Livingston was assigned to teach flying primary training at the Naval Air Station at Ottumwa, Iowa. Many cadet groups passed through primary training there, and Livingston made a profound impression on them. One young trainee named Richard Bach later gained notoriety by writing a very popular book entitled "Jonathan Livingston Seagull," a book about the ecstasy of flight and the importance of spiritual soaring and the drive to stretch your abilities to the limit. Published in 1970, it remains a classic today.

In the summer of 1939 the turmoil in Europe finally exceeded all bounds, and Germany began incorporating land masses of adjoining countries into its political boundaries. The futile peace negotiations resulted in open conflict, and England, France and other allies were forced to declare war on Germany to halt this aggressive expansion. America had adopted an isolationist position during this maneuvering, but many people recognized that ultimately America would be involved in some manner.

America was starting to experience a sense of relief and recovery from the trying times of the "great depression." Rural America was slower to respond, but there were more smiling faces and evidence of technological progress and opportunities for employment to buoy the human spirit. Progress in rural electrification, bank loans, affordable tractors and farm equipment, social advancement, and improved roads projected a better life for everyone.

And while this expression of positive change unfolded over our country, the certainty of war and the uncertainty of our future involvement cast a certain apprehension in families and on college campuses throughout the nation.

An Iowa Pilot Named Hap

CHAPTER FOUR
BASIC TRAINING

Attending college to become a coach meant exposure to many sports not offered in Grandview High School. Happy had lettered in basketball, played some baseball, but other sports were not offered. Teachers College required mandatory exposure to all sports offered in schools across Iowa. Happy went out for football his freshman year without previously having ever donned pads. His few weeks on the "meatball squad" emphasized one aspect of the game he was not familiar with. His five-foot-six-inch frame was better suited to individual competitive sports. He later tried wrestling, only to dislocate a shoulder. The classes made him participate in a variety of sports. His basic athleticism and hard work helped him understand the strategy and tactics of sports, and he displayed good progress toward a coaching profession.

Westbrook continued flying lessons with the Livingstons and was a quick learner in handling aircraft. Finally it was time for his cross-country solo flight. On a bright, clear morning, November 11th, 1940, Happy gathered his flight gear and climbed into the Taylorcraft. The preflight inspection completed, he strapped in and taxied to the end of the runway.

He would be taking off into a stiff breeze from the northwest on his three-leg flight, and he noticed a few clouds on the horizon. Airborne, he flew an hour and twenty minutes to his first checkpoint, then turned to align the compass toward checkpoint two, when a blast of freezing rain and wet snow hit the plane. He continued to checkpoint two amidst snow flurries and gusting winds. Turning on the home leg the snow increased, and visibility reduced to several hundred feet. He managed to control the buffeting airplane, arrived at the Waterloo Airport, and touched down on a barely discernible runway. Sixty mile per hour gusts of wind shook the plane as Westbrook taxied to the sheltered side of a hangar. He leapt out and immediately tied down the plane.

The storm of Armistice Day 1940 became a legendary storm with six foot snowdrifts, strong gusty winds, and below zero temperatures that brought most of Iowa to a complete halt for three days. Westbrook's instructors were awestruck that the fledgling pilot had survived the severity of the storm. In late November, without ceremony, Hartley Westbrook received his pilot's certificate signed by Jonathan Livingston.

The euphoria of completing his first flying experience, dating a really neat girl, and generally having a wonderful college experience was suddenly shattered on Sunday afternoon, December 7th, 1941. Happy and his fraternity brothers listened to reports on the radio, and studying was out of the question.

The next day, Teachers College students gathered at 11:00 a.m. around the radio in the college auditorium and listened somberly, sadly, as President Roosevelt stated, "Yesterday, December 7, 1941, a date which will live in infamy-The United States was suddenly and deliberately attacked by the naval and air forces of the Empire of Japan..."

The world had changed. America would change. The lives of the students at Teachers College would change in unimaginable ways.

The mobilization of some sort of military force had started earlier, with the Selective Service choosing numbers from a pail, committing young men to a year of military service. Registering for the "draft" was reluctantly complied with by the young men of the day, and particularly opposed by college students who wanted to complete their education. The draft proceeded slowly, but the events at Pearl Harbor changed all that. Each person was given a number that identified the group of young men to be called into service in the Army. It was apparent that Westbrook would have a fairly high draft number, and since his selection was imminent, he decided to take advantage of his CPT training. Westbrook volunteered for the Army Air Force at the end of the first quarter of his junior year. And Jane Bowers and Hartley Westbrook became much more serious in their relationship.

In January 1942, five young men from the Citizens Pilot Training class traveled to Fort Des Moines for induction. After induction, Cadet Houck, son of the postmaster at Guthrie Center, and Happy climbed into the four-door Ford and drove to Bakersfield, California, for processing. After a short period of time, they moved

Primary flight training at King City, CA, in Stearman P-22s. Photos showing the base were forbidden at that time.

to King City, CA, for primary training, flying Ryan and Stearman PT-22s. Since Happy had his license, he spent additional time studying military manuals and sharpened his flying skills.

After completing primary training in King City, the class moved to Moffit Air Force Base at San Jose, CA, for advanced training. Their class was the last army class at Moffit before it was turned over to the navy for flight training. It was an established base with several large aircraft hangers, one of which was built for lighter-than-air aircraft, or dirigibles, as they were once called.

The huge hangar was built to house Shenandoah or Los Angeles class airships, which were a part of the military at the time. A good deal of money and effort were expended developing airships, after Germany developed them in the 1910s and 20s for transcontinental flight. Their huge size, 680 feet long and 100 feet in diameter, seemed disproportionate to their passenger capacity of forty people and staff. Their speed of only sixty miles per hour, exposure to the elements, and flimsy construction would be their ultimate demise. The explosion of the Graf Hindenburg while tying up at an airfield in New Jersey in 1938 signaled the end of the big behemoths as a viable military consideration. However, inflatable rubber "blimps" were used for patrolling the west coast shores and searching for submarines.

The airship hangar size was immense. Approximately a thousand feet long and three hundred feet wide, the center reached a height of one hundred seventy-five feet. Open at the ends, it was

In January 2001, Hap revisited Moffitt Field and the lighter-than-air airship hangar that had challenged his flying ability during advanced training in 1942. Of course the big doors were open on that surprising day.

an imposing structure. It was also tempting to a young pilot on a training flight in a BT-13 single engine trainer. As maintenance crews inside the huge hangar busied themselves repairing aircraft, they were suddenly startled by a roaring BT-13 passing through the hangar at full throttle. They were so startled no one caught the aircraft identification numbers, and the young pilot could not be identified.

After several inquiries by the base staff, the search ended, but orders were issued threatening dismissal for any more recklessness.

Happy Westbrook showed mock surprise, but he had proven to his cadet classmates that it could be done.

It was here in primary training that Hartley's nickname "Happy" was shortened to "Hap," a name he would answer to for the rest of his life.

Actor Jimmy Stewart was at Moffit at that time and had been in the class immediately ahead of Westbrook's class. Because he was already a pilot his class time was abbreviated, and due to other complications he graduated in the 42-g class along with Westbrook.

Hap's byline in the Class 42-g graduation brochure said, "Westbrook, Hartley A...our dark-haired Romeo is as effective in a plane as in a drawing room...for real versatility note his technique in volley ball...he doesn't net a thing."

Jane graduated from Teachers College in the spring of 1941 and began interviewing with school districts. She accepted a teaching position in Napier and taught for one year. Hap, however, had other plans, and during her first year of teaching asked her to take a job where she could leave to join him at base assignments after he received his wings. They decided to get married as soon as Hap received his commission, without trepidation over what the future would hold during wartime years.

After teaching one year Jane found a job in Coon Rapids with an entrepreneur named Roswell Garst. Garst had several enterprises that included grocery stores, farm stores, and a fledging seed corn company. Jane served as a personal secretary, worked in the grocery store, and helped keep books. Garst often spent the night on a couch in back of the store, sleeping in his underwear, and Jane would wake him in the morning, serving hot coffee. Jane continued to work for Garst until she received a most important phone call.

Garst became internationally famous because of his knowledge of corn genetics and seed corn development. On a trip to Russia during the cold war to explain his progress in corn genetics, he became friends with Nikita Khrushchev, the Russian Premiere, who was interested in Garst's contribution to improving corn production. Garst invited Khrushchev to visit his farm in Coon Rapids, and in September 1959, during a thirteen-day visit to the United States, he spent one day touring the farm. The event was a major international story and drew a good deal of attention to a small Iowa town.

After Moffit Air Base, the next training Westbrook received was at Chico Air Base outside Sacramento, California. Here they took advanced training, formation flying, and cross country flying. Their frequent training trips took them to northern California, San Francisco Bay and along the coast. One day while flying along the Pacific landfall, three planes were flying in formation when the lead pilot recognized the towers of the Golden Gate Bridge down the coast. With a span of eleven hundred feet and height of one hundred seventy five feet, it would certainly accommodate an AT-6 with a thirty-six foot wingspan. The planes dropped to an appropriate elevation and turned to fly under the bridge, from the bay toward the ocean. The fly-under incident was reported to the military by a casual observer. The military authorities were as concerned about security of the bridge as they were about the flying violation. Again it was impossible to find out who the perpetrators of such an event were. Sometime later one of the plane identity numbers was turned in, and the identified cadet was dismissed, without revealing the identity of the lead pilot or other pilot in the formation.

The cadets trained in AT6s, AT-7s, AT-8s and AT-11s whenever they were available. With the major influx of trainees, there were not enough training planes to meet the demand until several months later. There were numerous cross-country training flights. The AT-6s carried three pockets for parachute flares for use during nighttime emergency landings. It was common to remove two flares and insert bottles of Coke to drink while flying. There were reported incidents of the Coke bottles being dropped on trucks traveling the highway, but they were never confirmed. Rumors were, the incidence of accuracy was quite high.

Finally, on July 27, 1942, at Chico Air Base, the cadet class graduated. Hartley Westbrook received his pilot's wings and was commissioned in the Army Air Force as a Second Lieutenant, O-728041. He was given seven days to report to his next assignment. Hap immediately caught a ride to Des Moines, and was met at the airport by Jane's family.

On July 29th, at the First Methodist Church in Bayard, Iowa, Jane Bowers and Lieutenant Hartley Westbrook were married. It was a small, simple ceremony attended by family, a few flowers and a few friends. Jane's sister, Ethel, was maid of honor and Hap's brother, Frederick, was the best man. After a brief reception, Hap and Jane put their luggage in Hap's newly acquired '39 Ford Coupe and drove to Letts, where they spent several days with the Westbrook family. They then left for Oklahoma City and Wiley Post Airfield for a new assignment. The eight-day honeymoon would be the most time they would spend together for over two years.

America was at war, and across the land young service men and their lovers had to make every second count.

This wedding picture was taken July 29th, 1942 at the Bayard Methodist Church, after the ceremony. The picture shows best man Fredrick Westbrook, Hap, the Minister (Unidentified), Jane and bridesmaid Ethel Bowers, Jane's Sister.

An Iowa Pilot Named Hap

CHAPTER FIVE
ENGLAND

Wiley Post Airfield was a staging and assignment area for the Air Force, preparatory for overseas service. Jane and Hap lived on base in officers housing. Hap was assigned a crew and they flew their first B-24 Liberator bomber. Flying the four engine aircraft was a totally different experience than the one and two engine trainers at Moffit.

Standing in front of their new '39 Ford Coupe, Hap and Jane prepare to leave for Hap's new assignment in Oklahoma City, prior to going overseas.

Hap was temporarily attached to the Barksdale, Louisiana, airfield that contained a unit assigned to fly submarine patrols over the Gulf of Mexico. In a brief time Hap managed to get twenty-one hours in the cockpit as a co-pilot, flying B-24s in search of submarines. This also gave him a rating as an experienced pilot, assigning him additional duties.

Oklahoma in August in Army housing without air conditioning was not the ideal honeymoon. But the hours between classes, briefing and assignments were shared with Jane and became precious moments. Time was spent anticipating future assignments, and developing a code for communicating locations when censoring would not permit identifying bases. Perhaps the best news was, as an officer and a gentleman, Hap would receive a whole $350 per month. In those days it was a lot of money, particularly to an Iowa farm boy who was used to walking along side a cultivator for fifty cents per day plus horse feed, horses included.

Hap was finally assigned to the 67th squadron of the 44th bomb group late in August. The 44th also contained the 66th, 68th and later, the 506th bomb squadrons. They would be flying a newly developed bomber, the B-24 Liberator. The plane was larger than the popular Boeing B-17, which had received a good deal of publicity when first introduced to the military.

In 1938 Consolidated Aircraft, later known as Convair, was asked to design a heavy bomber with performance characteristics exceeding the B-17. The new plane was designed using a new wing configuration developed by Consolidated that had improved lifting capacity. The new bomber looked so promising that thirty-one were ordered before the first one ever flew. B-24s were later manufactured by Douglas, Ford and North American, as well as Consolidated, and 18,481 planes were built, more than any other military aircraft in history. It was the only combat aircraft used in every theater of operations during WW II. The new wing configuration, narrower in width than the B-17, gave it better lift, but had less stability in level flight during bombing runs. It was 25 miles per hour faster than a B-17 at 290 MPH, had a larger bomb capacity of 8,800 pounds, and had a greater range, 1,590 miles. However, its lines were not as graceful as the "Flying Fortress," and B-17 pilots called it the "box they brought our plane over in."

A squadron contained twelve planes, but initially only eight planes were available for the 67th squadron. Without a full contingent of planes the flight crews had to rotate practice flights. Since the plane was new there was no instruction manual, no directions, not much feedback from units that were using them, and it was a whole new learning experience. As the first Liberator bombers in England, their bombing missions became empirical standards for future missions. It was learning on the job, under the worst conditions.

Overseas orders were finally cut, and the 44th bomb group was assigned to England. Second Lieutenant Westbrook was the officer delegated to accompany the maintenance crews via water to their new location. Westbrook met with the maintenance crews, and in early September boarded a train for New Jersey to the embarkation point.

Jane and two other wives went to the station to say goodbye, but also to verify which direction the train was headed. They trailed it out of town, and when it headed east, they bought train tickets

CONSOLIDATED B-24 LIBERATOR

Gross weight: 64,500 lbs. Span: 110' Length: 67'-2" Engine: 4-Pratt & Whitney R-1830-65 Armament: 10 - .50 Browning machine-guns Crew: 9 Speed: 290 mph at 25,000 ft. Ceiling: 28,000 ft.

Hartley "Hap" Westbrook

east, in order to spend as much time with their husbands as possible. They actually passed the troop train in Pittsburgh, and went on to New York City, where Jane stayed with a friend. Jane and Hap managed to spend another day together, as the maintenance crews boarded the Queen Mary for their trip to England.

Once boarded, the Queen Mary left the New Jersey dock and New York Harbor area, and joined a convoy for England. The second night out Hap joined other officers in the Officers Mess, enjoying an evening scotch, when the ship shuddered and shook violently. The BBC radio in the wardroom announced, "The Queen Mary has been torpedoed by German submarines." In reality, the convoy had detected submarines in the area, and since the Queen Mary had the speed to outrun underwater craft, it shuddered when it increased to "full steam ahead." Fortunately, the BBC was incorrect, and the Queen Mary proceeded ahead of the convoy and a few days later landed in Glasgow, Scotland.

The maintenance crew proceeded by train to their new station at Shipdham, in central northwest England. With the influx of airplanes anticipated, there was a massive construction program to fulfill the need for landing 80,000 pound aircraft. Before WW II, there were only two hundred active airfields in England. Five hundred additional airfields were built to house the sixty heavy bomber groups, fifteen medium bomber groups and twenty-five fighter groups to be stationed there. The quantity of concrete used in constructing these airfields was the equivalent of four thousand miles of three lane highways. U.S. Army Engineer Battalions were brought in to complete construction on designs established by English civil engineers. In East Anglia, the large concentration of airfields and personnel came to be known as "Little America."

The airfields assumed a standardized form of construction of three overlapping runways in a triangle form with the major windward runway about 6,000 feet long. The other two runways were approximately 4,200 feet long. A taxiway fifty foot wide encircled the entire runway system, and from that, dispersal nodes containing three circular hardstands for parking the aircraft. Enclosed hangars, housing, operations headquarters, and a two-story control tower completed the basic installation. A bomb storage depot and

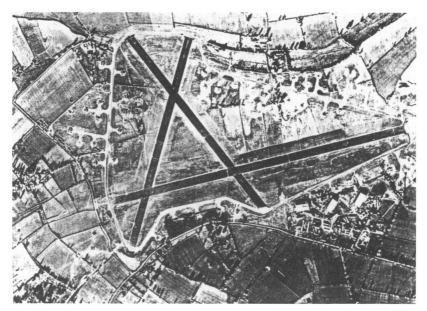

Early picture of the airfield at Shipdham, home of the 67th, 66th and 68th squadrons of the 44th Bomb Group. Three runways and taxiways located on the Patterson Farm were typical construction. One-story living units were dispersed around the perimeter. (photo: Fields of Little America)

service area were more remote. In 1942 a new airfield was started every three days, and work continued until the facility was complete. Each airfield was self-contained with general staff, communications, maintenance personnel, and crews for thirty-six aircraft. Also, each airfield had their own IOF for identifying their field when returning from missions.

Because of the speed of construction, the airfields consisted of concrete and exposed dirt. Of course in the English weather the dirt became mud and almost never dried out. When on missions the airplanes took off at thirty-second intervals. Occasionally, a plane turning onto the runway would have one wheel slip into the mud, and the weight of the plane would cause it to become mired. As a result, the remaining flights would have to abort, since access to the runway was not possible. It was distressing since some squadrons would be undermanned in resisting attacking German fighter planes, and the potential to reduce a target to rubble substantially reduced. Those crews who had to abort were grateful, since they

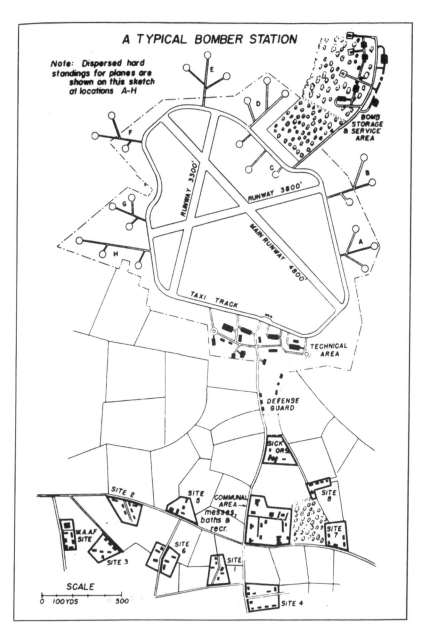

Typical layout of the many airfields built to accommodate the incoming American bomber groups. Runways, dispersal, hangars and maintenance, and housing were scattered to avoid occasional visits from the German Luftwaffe. (photo: Airfields of the Eighth)

were spared the exposure to shrapnel from anti-aircraft guns and visits from unfriendly Messerschmitts.

One must consider the considerable pressure placed on the British people, creating hundreds of airfields for the thousands of airplanes and men to arrive. America's early commitment for material and military support for England was encouraged by President Roosevelt, but our Congress could not act since America was not at war. Through the "Lend Lease" effort the U.S. furnished much non-military material and food in support of Britain. The attack on Pearl Harbor changed all that, and full commitment lagged until production could furnish the planes, ammunition, bombs and young men that were needed for the task at hand.

As soon as the squadron arrived from the United States, they assembled in Shipdham and commenced active preparation and training. Hap was assigned as co-pilot to a plane named "Miss Dianne." One of the first responsibilities was to fly to Ireland to install armament. Initially the bombers were to be defended with

.30 caliber machine guns which were changed to .50 caliber for more killing power. Early machine guns fired at 300 rounds per minute (RPM), and the new guns could deliver 3000 RPM at enemy aircraft, a decided improvement.

While the installation was in progress, the crew went to a nearby pub to taste the local flavor. Hap was now sporting a pencil mustache, the only facial hair permitted by the Air Force, and he cut quite a figure in his "pink and greens."

About that time actor Clark Gable enlisted in the Army Air Force and was given a captain's commission. In order to encourage enlistments as waist gunners, which were in short supply, Gable volunteered to

This photo of Hap taken after the war, with his pencil moustache, shows how he could have been mistaken for Clark Gable by soldiers stationed in Ireland. At five-foot-six-inches tall, Westbrook was five inches shorter than Gable, but that did not deter the airmen who were certain it was Gable.

serve in that capacity, to lend glamour and thus increase enlistments. Word soon spread that Gable was in England reporting for duty. As Westbrook and his crew left the Irish pub, an enlisted man spotted the mustachioed Lieutenant and shouted, "There's Gable!" Immediately a line of thirty or so enlisted men formed, each waiving a dollar bill for "Gable" to sign. Although it would have been fun to hoodwink the young men, it took considerable discussion to convince those present he was not the famous actor.

It was later learned the Germans picked up on the rumor, and a bonus was offered to German fighter pilots to shoot down Gable in order to influence America's morale.

One bomber returning from Ireland after servicing started vibrating severely, and the pilot and co-pilot could not get the airplane under control. Not wanting to lose their airplane, they made an emergency landing on a sod farm field in central England. The length of the field did not permit developing enough speed to clear the fences and trees to return to the base.

Lieutenant Westbrook was given the task to retrieve the airplane. Westbrook, a co-pilot and an engineer were trucked to the site to review the possibilities.

The soft soil inhibited building speed needed for liftoff. After checking out the aircraft to determine the cause of excessive vibration, they devised a plan for getting the bomber out of the farm field. They taxied to one end of the field, and started down wind at full throttle. As they neared the fence, they executed a full speed u-turn and headed into the wind, gaining enough speed to lift the bomber over the field obstructions. It was a daring maneuver in the soft soil, but without the ingenuity and fortitude displayed by the crew, the plane would have had to be towed to the nearest airfield, not an easy task.

CHAPTER SIX
GETTING ACQUAINTED

The new B-24 was a solid plane, not nearly as glamorous as the B-17, but faster with greater range and more bomb capacity. Because it could fly at 28,000 feet (39,000 feet with turbo-chargers) it was necessary that each airman dress warmly, have oxygen, and be able to function in the minus 50 degree temperatures at that height. The gunner's hands froze, gun oil froze and metal equipment behaved differently in the extreme temperature. Later improvements in electrically heated flying suits improved performance, but hands still froze to metal, and inability to move about hindered activity. The least bit of over heating caused problems with comfort when trying to cool down. It took a good deal of study to find the proper mixture of oil on machine guns to keep them operable in cold weather. It was not uncommon for flights to be aborted because pilots did not want to risk engaging German fighter planes when their only defense, the machine guns, were frozen.

Each station aboard the airplane had a relief tube to use during the long flights, but use was limited by the extreme cold. Some airmen found it more convenient to use their metal helmets. Tail gunners and belly gunners were so cramped in their turrets that once in position, it was impossible to leave to urinate. As a result, they suffered from severe chafing and were constantly seeking medication. They were easy to identify from a distance because they "walked funny."

The plane was heavy, carrying 6,600 pounds of bombs as well as 6,000 pounds of ammunition. Each airman had a job to do and a responsibility to protect each other. It was the responsibility of the captain and co-pilot to know all of the other responsibilities, but once in flight, each person was individually responsible. Bombardiers, engineers and navigators doubled as machine gunners after their main task was done. An intercom let them talk among themselves, but there was radio silence between planes for security from German interception. They were a team with only two objectives: bomb the enemy and live to bomb another day.

The new arrivals in England were encouraged to meet and mix

with the local English people. As one of the first air contingents on the British Isles away from the major cities, the airmen were openly welcomed by the local citizens. The local command received an invitation for four officers (gentlemen of course) to visit Lord and Lady Bradley for an evening of bridge. Bridge was one of the main ways to pass time during basic and advance training, and was very popular at the time. Hap was an excellent bridge player, and the opportunity to mix with the local English was appealing. Hap responded to the invitation, gathered his navigator, bombardier and engineer, checked out a staff car and drove to the estate.

The Bradley's were most welcoming and generous with the few provisions they could get, and early on, most friendly with the new American visitors. The home resembled a castle, a beautiful structure on well laid out grounds with a long curving driveway. The airmen were treated to a wonderful meal, without certain basic foods, and shared Lord Bradley's last bottle of scotch. Lady Bradley noted that with the various shortages she had no soap, but was getting along just fine.

Westbrook made a mental note, and on their next invitation for a "shoot" presented the Bradley's with a case of shotgun shells, several bottles of scotch, soap and what food they could acquire. The Bradley's were most appreciative. When the airmen were leaving, Lord Bradley said, "Some day when you are about, as you Americans say, buzz me."

A few weeks later, Westbrook's squadron was used for a decoy flight. Early in the campaign, when the allies did not have air cover superiority and when a bombing mission was commenced, the Americans would send two bomber groups. One was the actual bombing mission, and the other flew in an alternate direction to draw fighter planes from the main group. The decoy group then circled and returned to England. On the return run Westbrook's plane was "burning down" fuel for a safer landing and decided to buzz Lord and Lady Bradley's estate. Dropping to a low altitude, cutting back airspeed, Hap circled the grounds and coasted over the castle at rooftop height. When he got over the house, he pushed the throttles full forward and kicked in his four 1200 horsepower engines. With 4,800 horsepower, the plane violently shuddered and slowly climbed away.

Several weeks later, Westbrook and the officers were again invited to visit the Bradley's estate. As they approached the "castle" in their staff car, they noticed plywood over all the windows on one side of the house. When Hap inquired if they had been bombed, Lord Bradley replied, "We weren't bombed. Some bloody Yank flew low over the house and blew out all the windows on the west side!"

Westbrook and the men did their best to look shocked, and immediately changed the subject.

As the war progressed and more Americans flooded the tiny hamlets in East Anglia, the original hospitality dissipated, as one might expect. The English were still friendly, but less inclined to invite American soldiers into their homes. The service clubs and dance halls became the venue for interacting, and were popular with the airmen as well as the local patrons.

Lt. Westbrook at Shipdham Air Base in East Anglia.

The English weather became a major influence in operations. The weather was unpredictable, overcast, and foggy most of the time, which made flying hazardous to and from the target. When beginning an early morning mission, assembly over the North Sea was very difficult since radio silence and visibility made it difficult to find proper squadron formations. Occasionally, because of the fog, a plane would attach itself to the wrong squadron, and would continue with it rather than search for its proper position in the assigned squadron.

Operations experimented with garish paint schemes for the lead planes in a squadron, to assist visibility in assembling. The paint schemes helped identify squadron leaders, but in thick fog, poor visibility was the enemy.

Early in the campaign, the learning curve for bombing crews was not only time-consuming and fear-inducing, but incredibly expensive in terms of airplanes and crews.

SQUADRON ASSEMBLY IDENTIFICATION

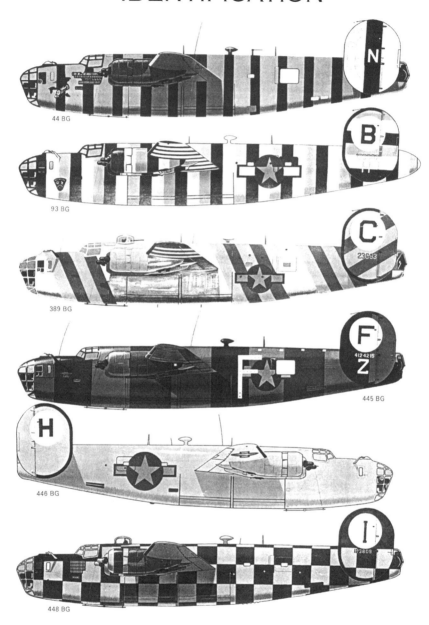

Special marking to identify bomber groups during inclement weather and fog. Yellow was the predominant color. (Photo: The Mighty Eighth)

An Iowa Pilot Named Hap

CHAPTER SEVEN
MISSIONS

The 67th squadron continued to prepare for being inserted into the bombing rotation.

The crew of "Miss Dianne" consisted of Clyde Price as captain and first pilot, Westbrook as second pilot, Second Lieutenant Jacob Augenstene navigator, Second Lieutenant Morton Gross bombardier, Staff Sergeant Iris Wyer, Jr. radio operator/gunner, Tech Sergeant Kenneth Laughton radio operator/gunner, Tech Sergeant Dalton Snell engineer/top turret gunner, Staff Sergeant Norman Breniser engineer/top turret gunner, Staff Sergeant Kenneth Erheard waist gunner, Staff Sergeant Lewis Fleshman tail gunner, and Staff Sergeant Roy Gosline rear hatch gunner.

The camaraderie of a crew was short lived. As missions started, and loss of planes and personnel escalated, crews were hastily put together and operating planes re-assigned in order to get the required number of aircraft in the air for a specific target. The 44th Bomb Group had inordinate losses from early on, as they were learning on the job. Fighter planes with limited range accompanied the bombers to the mainland coast, and the bombers were then escorted the remaining distance to the target and back by Messerschmitts and Focke-Wulfs.

There were many heroics as the 44th BG did its best to carry out its missions, and they ultimately experienced over eighty-eight

Captain Clyde Price, first pilot, standing in front of the "Miss Dianne" B-24 Liberator Bomber. Note the "Flying Eightballs" insignia and row of bombs denoting four bombing missions.

Photograph taken during the May 14th mission to Keil, Germany. Westbrook is flying the distant plane with the tail marking L. (photo: US Air Force)

percent losses. The unit became known as the "Flying Eightballs," and a special insignia was designed with a black eight ball with a bomb penetrating it. They were recognized for their heroics when on May 14th, 1943 twenty-one B-24s joined over a hundred B-17s to fly a mission to the Kiel Submarine base in northern Germany. The flack was terrific, along with swarms of enemy fighters and in the ensuing engagement, the bomb group destroyed thirty-two planes, five probably destroyed, and one damaged. The mission included planes from the 66th, 68th, 506th and three planes from the 67th. This effort gained them their first Distinguished Unit Citation. The group commander, Colonel Leon Johnson, was later posthumously awarded America's highest medal, the Congressional Medal of Honor, for the raid on the Polesti Oil Fields.

While training, the squadron was often used as a diversionary group, to get the "feel" of actual missions. They were exposed to some anti-aircraft fire and fighter planes, but most flights were uneventful. Some missions were aborted, and did not count as a "combat mission" per se. Soon they were involved on a regular basis.

The first 44th Group mission took place November 7th, 1942, (Mission 1). It was a diversionary mission over the North Sea to Cape De La Hague and back again.

MISSIONS THAT HAP WESTBROOK PARTICIPATED IN WERE:

December 6th, 1942, Mission 6, as co-pilot aboard the "Suzy Q." The target was the Abbeville-Drucat Airdrome at Abbeville, France. It included six planes from the 68th, seven planes from the 67th, and six planes from the 68th squadron. A recall was issued and planes from the 66th and 67th returned to the base. The 68th, unaware of the recall, continued to the target dropping its bombs, but losing one plane.

January 3rd, 1943, Mission 9, co-pilot aboard "Miss Dianne." The target was the ship building port and torpedo storage facilities at St. Nazaire, France.

January 27th, 1943, Mission 10, co-pilot aboard "Miss Marcia Ann" to Lemmer, Holland. The original targets were submarine building yards at Wilhelmshaven, Germany - the first mission into Germany. The weather conditions were terrible, and flying over the North Sea the attack force got lost, never reaching Germany. An alternate target was selected and bombs were dropped on "targets of opportunity."

February 4th, 1943, Mission 11, co-pilot aboard "Miss Dianne." The Mission to Hamm Germany was recalled due to inclement weather that froze machine guns and oxygen masks.

February 15th, 1943, Mission 12, co-pilot aboard "Miss Dianne." The target was a German raider ship docked at Dunkirk, France, a hastily called mission to respond to reconnaissance sightings. The ship, the Tojo, was a technically advanced cruiser disguised as a slow cargo ship. It would approach Allied shipping and get close enough to inflict great damage to the unsuspecting convoys. Twelve planes were involved in the bombing run, but the port was heavily defended, and only four planes returned, one of them "Miss Dianne."

On this mission Hap lost his best friend in service, Ed Wilks, from Tennessee. They had met the first week at induction into the Air Force and gone through flight school together.

February 27th, 1943, Mission 15, co-pilot aboard "Miss Dianne." The target was the seaport and U-boat pens at Brest, France.

March 4th, 1943, Mission 16, co-pilot aboard "Miss Dianne" was a diversion mission to Frisian Islands along the coast of Holland.

March 6th, 1943, Mission 17, co-pilot aboard the "Miss Dianne." Target St. Nazaire, France. Miss Dianne was credited with five enemy aircraft destroyed, and in turn suffered major damage requiring thirty-six hours to repair.

March 8th, 1943, Mission 18, co-pilot aboard the "Suzy Q." Target was the marshalling yards at Rouen, France. The bomber formation was attacked by 30 to 40 German Focke-Wulf 190 fighter planes that were visually mistaken for American P-47s. The two lead B-24s were shot down, and the remaining planes abandoned the primary target and dropped their bombs on 'targets of opportunity."

April 4th, 1943, Mission 25, co-pilot aboard the "Suzy Q." This mission was a diversionary mission from Orfordness to North Foreland, to assist fortresses attacking Antwerp, Belgium.

April 5th, 1943, Mission 26, co-pilot aboard the "Suzy Q." Target was a truck parts plant in Antwerp, Belgium.

May 1, 1943, Mission 28, co-pilot aboard the "Bela/Beck's Bad Boys." Diversionary mission.

May 4th, 1943, Mission 29, co-pilot aboard the "Bela/Beck's Bad Boys." Diversionary Mission.

May 14th, 1943, Mission 30, pilot aboard the "Miss Delores." Target was the Krupp Submarine Works, Kiel, Germany.

Maintenance crews worked around the clock to keep planes available for combat. Their attachment to a specific crew was short lived, because of the turnover in lost aircraft. When damaged aircraft did make it back to the base, it was put in the "junk pile" and parts were salvaged for reuse or replacement. Maintenance crews were quite ingenious in adapting the airplanes to improvements suggested by returning crews. Occasionally the maintenance men would have an opportunity to slip into town and quaff a few beers at Kingshead Pub or Golden Dog Pub on High Street in Shipdham. But mostly they had their hands full servicing the aircraft to keep them in flying condition.

Early in the campaign air protection for the bombers was furnished by the English in Spitfires, a very adequate fighter plane but without much range. Later, the P-47s were introduced and had a sterling record, but again their range was limited. It was only when the P-51 Mustangs with wing tanks were introduced that bomber protection was adequate. By that time, the Allies had air superiority, and German fighters, in short supply, avoided confronting the superior force. Early bombing runs invariably accounted for several German fighter planes being shot down. In a massive bombing raid one hundred or more German fighters might rise to protect the Reich. Late in the war bomber pilots would complete fifty missions and be challenged by fighter planes only a few times.

German anti-aircraft guns were mobile, and when a target was hit several times protection was moved about. Bomb groups often flew at different heights to out-fox the German artillery, but the Germans were quite accurate in creating a shield of shrapnel. The result of their "protection" was surprising. Pilots talked of flying on "carpets of flak."

The 44th Bomb Group, or "Eightballs," left a number of records behind them. They operated from England longer, made more missions, and claimed more enemy fighters than any other B-24 Liberator group. In their 343 missions, the group lost 153 aircraft, each with a crew of ten.

By the war's end, over 118,000 airmen were killed, wounded or missing, and some 48,000 of those became prisoners of war.

As replacement planes arrived, improvements in equipment were made. New technology produced the NDB (Non Directional Beacon) and the ADF (Automatic Direction Finder). They helped immeasurably in coping with the English weather.

The English believed in night bombing. The Americans thought you could bomb during working hours of daylight. Both set out to prove the other wrong, which turned out to be an advantage, since it kept the Germans active in defense both day and night. Americans were up early at 4:00 a.m. or 5:00 a.m., had breakfast and were in the briefing room at 6:00 a.m. Targets were identified, weather conditions described, planes assigned, crews shuffled and final instructions given. An hour or so later, they were in their planes awaiting takeoff. Arrival time at the target invariably interrupted the German's lunch hour.

At the American crew's breakfast of eggs, bacon toast and coffee, the crews talked about the job they had to do, and avoided discussing losses, planes down or friends missing. They usually flew two missions a week and spent the other days in the classroom studying evasive techniques, evacuation drills, formation flying and mechanical equipment. They also shared information learned on previous missions.

In March 1943, Hartley Westbrook was promoted to First Lieutenant. He was frequently asked to fill in with other crews and his performance level was noted. On May 1st he was promoted to Captain in the U.S. Army Air Force, a promotion he was not aware of until his release from the prisoner of war camp.

The submarine menace in the North Atlantic continued to inflict severe damage to Allied shipping and efforts to get strategic materials to England. Allied strategy was to take steps to severely curtail the construction, servicing and supplying of the underwater craft. The German submarine bases along the North Sea coast at Kiel, Germany, and Brest, France, were well prepared to resist intrusion. The roof construction consisted of twelve feet of reinforced concrete. In addition, numerous anti-aircraft batteries were deployed to protect the bases from attacks in any direction. Several fighter airbases were established in close proximity with the capability of putting over a hundred aircraft in the air to defend the bases.

Many types of bombs were used by the Allies to try to demolish the bases, including five hundred pound bombs, cluster bombs and incendiary bombs. Had the bombs been dropped at the right location, they might have been effective, but getting to the target proved to be most difficult.

On May 14th, a massive raid on Kiel was planned. Twenty-four Liberators were scheduled to join the hundred plus B-17s assigned to the mission. The intent of the raid was for the B-17s to "bomb the hell out of the U-boat pens, aircraft factories and seaport facilities." The B-24s carried incendiary bombs to kindle the fires. Last minute problems in another bomb group reduced the number of participating Liberators to nineteen from the 44th BG.

Lieutenant Robert Brown, pilot of the "Suzy Q," was to pilot the plane, "Miss Delores," and Westbrook was to fly as copilot. However a last minute switch by Brown put Westbrook in the pilot seat and Brown in the co-pilot seat. Miss Delores was assigned as the last plane in the Liberator formation, the most dangerously exposed location in the formation.

Normally, the Liberators flew higher than the Fortresses and bombed through their formations. On the Kiel mission, the high command dictated the Liberators would reduce speed and fly behind the B-17s. This posed a problem, since B-17s cruised at 160 MPH and the Liberators cruised at 185 indicated air speed. The stall speed for Liberators carrying a full load of bombs was about 160 MPH.

The Liberators assembled over Cromer at 21,000 feet and rendezvoused fifty miles further with the B-17s, who were stacked upwards to 32,000 feet. The B-24s had to zigzag forty miles in order to remain behind the Fortresses and not overtake them because of their slower speed. The Liberators were scheduled to go over the target at 21,000 feet, but because of zigzagging, were off course at 19,000 feet. The 44th's cargo of incendiaries required a shorter trajectory, longer bomb run, and a scattered formation, and was more exposed to fighter attack. Before they had time to release their bombs, five Liberators were shot down, three of them from the 67th squadron.

The Kiel mission was Westbrook's seventeenth mission, if you counted the five aborts. The good feeling of his first opportunity to be chief pilot was short lived. The anti-aircraft fire suddenly blossomed and a group of yellow-nosed Focke-Wulf 190s made a pass at the tail end formation. The first cannon blast in the tail section of the Miss Delores killed rear hatch gunner Sergeant Cate, tail gunner Staff Sergeant Klingler, and waist gunner Staff Sergeant Milhousen of the make up crew. Fortunately none of the incendiaries were ignited. Two engines were knocked out, and engine four trailed flames. Westbrook and Brown dropped the bomb bay doors and jettisoned their bombs.

Knowing they had a crippled plane, the FW-190s made another pass. The instrument panel was shattered, and Westbrook was shot in the right shoulder and shrapnel tore up his right leg, spilling blood inside his flying suit. Tech Sergeants Wandtke and Susan, and Staff Sergeant Ulrich strapped on chutes and dropped out of the bomb bay doors. Navigator Bishop, who was in the nose of the plane with Bombardier Hayward, saw a fighter bearing down on them and shouted "Duck!" Hayward was struck in the face with fragments, and Bishop had paint on his steel helmet stripped and scarred. They dropped through the nose wheel bay where Bishop frantically groped for his ripcord but could not find it. In his haste to snap on the British chest chute, he had put it on upside down. He fell to five thousand feet and finally found the release. Falling at 120 MPH, the impact of the chute opening sent his flying boots spinning off.

Brown finally found his parachute and dropped out of the plane's bomb bay. Westbrook tried to control the crippled plane as best he could, but it continued its slow spiral out to sea. He dropped thirty inches to the deck and found his parachute. His chute was riddled with shrapnel. He struggled to get it on and snap the straps in place. He found one of the crew perched at the bomb bay doors and shoved him off the plane. Hap did not know if the crewman was wearing a parachute, and carried that fear with him for years until he later learned that the crewman, as well as the remaining crew members, were POWs.

It was about one o'clock when Westbrook left the airplane. The attack and subsequent actions had lasted only a few minutes, but by now the airplane, in uncontrolled circular descent, was well out to sea. Engine number three continued to sputter, smoke filled the plane and the smell of hot oil burned his nostrils. He was sweating intensely from trying to hold the plane on course and moving around the deck, and was aware of the blood soaking his clothing. One last look, and he dropped out of the bomb bay doors. "Miss Delores," so dutifully serviced by the maintenance crew, would not survive this mission.

Westbrook fell a short distance, and with his disabled arm managed to jerk the ripcord. The chute, even with numerous holes, jerked Westbrook violently, and the oxygen container strapped to his leg flew away, pulling the mouthpiece out of his mouth along with two teeth. The jolt also popped his ears, and the intense silence frightened him. The airplane continued on its erratic descent for several miles, then suddenly burst into flames and exploded, carrying three young machine gunners to burial at sea.

Westbrook began to swing wildly from a strong cross wind, and he attempted desperately to stabilize his descent by pulling his side harness straps. He remembered safety lectures on the days between flights, and instructions to pop the safety harness just prior to hitting the water so as not to be pulled under water by the parachute. He twisted the release and hit it several times but it refused to let go. The failure of the release was for the best, since in his enthusiasm to practice a safe landing he was still several hundred feet in the air.

The Baltic Sea is a treacherous sea. Because of the winds, waves were cresting at six or seven feet. Hap's parachute continued to oscillate, and approaching the water's surface, he swung parallel with the horizon and dropped straight down on his face. The impact forced the release of his harness rig and his parachute floated beyond reach.

His first impulse was to curl up under water and kick off his fleece lined flying boots. When wet they would function as lead weights, or at least restrict movement. After several futile attempts he managed to get the zippers down and they floated away. He then pulled the charger on his Mae West, an air filled rubberized floating device, only to find that one-half of the vest had a bullet hole through it. The cold salt water cauterized his wounds, and although the pain was severe, cleansed the wounds. He had no feeling in his mouth from the lost teeth.

He struggled to get to the top of a wave only to crash to the bottom trough. After several attempts he was totally exhausted and finally bobbed along as the Baltic Sea dictated. His energy and effort had protected him from the icy water, but after a few moments, he felt the rapid loss of body warmth, then freezing cold and violent shivering, and ever so slowly, he drifted into unconsciousness.

CHAPTER EIGHT
KRIEGSGEFANGENER

Hypothermia is a rapid loss of body temperature. Several timeframes have been quoted for death by immersion in the North Sea or Baltic Sea during winter temperatures. It is generally agreed that twenty to thirty minutes is well beyond what the human body can endure. Hartley Westbrook parachuted into the water at about one o'clock in the afternoon. Late that afternoon, if dusk can be defined on a gray cloudy day, a large fishing boat spotted a bobbing object and presumed it to be another downed airman. They had retrieved two already, one who was rescued almost immediately after hitting the water, and one who had been dead for several hours. The large fishing boat of Swedish origin came about and the crew pulled the young airman on board. They presumed they were fishing another lifeless body from the Baltic Sea, but when they lifted him on deck were surprised to detect a very weak pulse.

They immediately took him below deck to the boiler room, stripped off his clothes and laid him on a table between two huge coal fired boilers. The temperature was probably between 120 and 130 degrees, and the noise intense. They intended to raise Hap's body temperature slowly, since he was exposed to water below 32 degrees because of the high salt content. There were no medical personnel aboard the ship, so no vital statistics could be checked. His wounds were treated casually, since the possibility of survival was presumed to be quite remote.

After several hours Westbrook slowly gained consciousness and his head cleared. He was aware of the loud noise, and workmen gathered around the table speaking in some strange tongue. The temperature was very hot and he was naked, lying on a table. His immediate thought was, "I HAVE DIED AND GONE TO HELL!"

The crewmen dressed his wounds, wrapped him in woolen blankets, and served him hot soup. Through gestures they let him know they were happy to have saved the doomed pilot. They delivered his dry uniform, and as he dressed he discovered his .45 caliber sidearm and $3000 cash were missing. The money was to be used as bribe money should he be shot down in enemy territory.

One of the crew who knew a little German and less English stepped forward and said, "Du sind ein Kriegsgefangener. For you the war is over."

As it later was proved, Westbrook's shooting war was over, but his war to survive had just begun.

There were two other airmen on board. One airman was in much better shape than Westbrook, and the other was wrapped in canvas on the foredeck. To protect the ship from German intervention and retaliation, the ship proceeded immediately to a German port and turned their guests over to authorities. They made port well after midnight, and German medics immediately dressed Hap's wounds. The two airmen were then trucked to a large country barn filled with straw, joining about twenty other airmen who on that fateful day had become "Kreigsgefangener."

The next morning, the officers in the captured group were assembled and transported to Berlin, then to Dulag Luft, at Oberorsal, a military facility for interrogating prisoners. Westbrook was placed in a five-by-eight-foot room and kept in isolation for a day. The following morning he was visited by a Luftwaffe officer, carrying a manila folder in his hand. When questioned about his base, target and other pertinent information, Hap followed the rules of the Geneva Convention on War, and responded with the proper name, rank and serial number.

The Luftwaffe officer then opened the folder and said, "How is your wife Jane? Didn't you meet her at Iowa State Teachers College? How was your trip over on the Queen Mary?" Other questions revealed the Germans had considerable knowledge about Hartley Westbrook's personal life. Hap often wondered about the source of this information. He spent one week in isolation while they tried to break down his composure and gain intelligence information, but Hap held steadfast to the Geneva Convention.

The prisoners were separated by rank as officers, non-commissioned officers and privates for distribution to different camps. Air Force officers were placed in camps controlled by the Luftwaffe at the command of Field Marshall Hermann Goering, the ranking German Air Officer. The American officers were loaded aboard a train and taken to a newly built camp about eighty miles from Berlin at Sagan, Poland, called Stalag Luft III.

HAP'S P.O.W. REGISTRATION

Personalkarte I: Personelle Angaben

Kriegsgefangenen-Stammlager: Stalag Luft 3

Name: W E S T B R O O K

Vorname: Hartley A.

Geburtstag und -ort: 29.1.19 Letts Iowa

Religion: Me.

Vorname des Vaters:

Familienname der Mutter:

Staatsangehörigkeit: USA

Dienstgrad: 1.Lt.

Truppenteil: USAAF   Kom. usw.:

Zivilberuf: Berufs-Gr.:

Matrikel Nr. (Stammrolle des Heimatstaates): 0-728.041

Gefangennahme (Ort und Datum): Eckernförde 14.5.43

Ob gesund, krank, verwundet eingeliefert:

Nähere Personalbeschreibung

Besondere Kennzeichen:

Grösse: 1,68   Haarfarbe: d.braun

Fingerabdruck des rechten I Zeigefingers

Lichtbild

Name und Anschrift der zu benachrichtigenden Person in der Heimat des Kriegsgefangenen

Mrs. Westbrook
57,H. Coon Rapids
LETTS, IOWA

Beschriftung der Erkennungsmarke

Nr.1319

Lager: Stalag Luft 3

Wenden!

Des Kriegsgefangenen

Personalkarte I for Stalag Luft III, Haps original Prisoner of War Registration card.

Jane Westbrook had this picture taken in Muscatine and sent it to Hap while he was a POW. Hap included this picture in his POW Logbook.

CHAPTER NINE
TELEGRAMS

Jane rolled and tossed in her sleep. She was not feeling well, her stomach uneasy, and she restlessly tried to find a comfortable sleeping position. She knew something was wrong, but could not focus on it. She finally drifted off and slept well past a schoolteacher's normal rising time. This Saturday morning she was at her home on the farm, sleeping in her schoolgirl bed. The flowered wallpaper was muted in the shaded light. The bookcases with childhood books and dolls and high school trivia were somehow soothing in Hap's absence.

About 9:30 a.m., her mother entered the room and shook her gently and said, "Jane, Mr. Dollarhyde is here from the telegraph office. He has a telegram for you."

Jane sat up and said quietly, "Yes, I know. Hap is missing."

The telegraph was terse. "THE SECRETARY OF WAR DESIRES ME TO EXPRESS HIS DEEP REGRET THAT YOUR HUSBAND FIRST LIEUTENANT HARTLEY WESTBROOK AIR FORCE HAS BEEN REPORTED MISSING IN ACTION SINCE MAY 14, 1943. ADDITIONAL INFORMATION WILL BE SENT WHEN RECEIVED."

The family was stunned receiving the news. It was a common misconception that bombers were above the battleground, and not involved in a shooting war. The possibility of losing Hap was remote, because "it only happens to other families, not ours." The optimism of youth is immortality. An early death, a chance death, or sudden accident is only a casual deterrent to the comfort of youthful immortality.

Ed Bowers was extremely fond of his son-in-law. He walked to the bench next to the pump house, slumped down, and quietly sobbed for half an hour.

Ethel Bowers tried to console Jane, but Jane was stoic in facing this reality. Had she and Hap discussed this on their trip to Oklahoma City? Had they even considered Jane becoming a war widow a possibility? Jane's response was completely controlled since she knew that Hap was still alive. Deep inside, it was only a hope.

Jane called Hap's parents and relayed the message. She then packed her clothes, and drove the Ford Coupe to Letts, to console Benjamin and Mabel on the loss of their son. The drive gave her an opportunity to sort through her emotions and develop a firm resolve. She knew Hap was alive. She stayed in Letts for about a week before returning to her job in Coon Rapids.

Jane had continued to work for Roswell Garst, rather than teach school, so she would be free to join Hap on short notice without violating a teacher's contract. She had written letters to Hap twice a week, but seldom heard back because of the rigors of Hap's duties. Mr. Garst was very understanding and kept Jane busy in several of his enterprises to keep her active and limit time for worrying.

About three weeks later, Jane went to work on a bright June morning at Garst's retail store in Coon Rapids. On the cash register keys was an envelope left by Mr. Dollarhyde.

It was a telegram from the International Red Cross.

"YOUR HUSBAND FIRST LIEUTENANT HARTLEY WESTBROOK AIR FORCE IS REPORTED A PRISONER OF WAR OF THE GERMAN GOVERNMENT."

Jane knew all along that Hap was alive.

One of the first letters she received from Hap in prison camp was a request for shoes, since he had lost his flying boots, and was making do with a mix-matched pair of shoes picked up along the way. What he really wanted was a pair of farm boots, or "Lil' Abner Boots" to withstand the rigors of prison camp. Jane immediately drove to Des Moines to the Army /Navy store and purchased a pair of officer dress shoes. They were packed in the "official size" box, and the remainder of the box stuffed full with soap, toothpaste and vitamins. The newly purchased dress shoes proved to be a problem later in Hap's POW experience.

She continued to write Hap twice a week. She did not know where he was located, writing to an Army Post Office (APO) in

New York. Prisoners were permitted to write one postcard per month, and Hap's post cards were often blacked out over fifty percent by suspicious camp censors. The German censors were overly cautious about concealing information in both incoming and outgoing letters. For the prisoners, receiving mail, even though half censored, was still an enormous morale booster.

That fall, Jane started teaching in the Bayard school system. She continued to live at home, on the farm with her parents.

In October of 1943, Jane received a phone call from the Air Force asking her to come to Des Moines for a presentation. Mr. and Mrs. Westbrook and Mr. and Mrs. Bowers also were asked to participate, and were accompanied by Mr. and Mrs. Alva Wagner, of Richland, Hap's grandparents, Dr. and Mrs. R.M. Irwin of Richland, Iowa, Hap's uncle and aunt, and Ethel Bowers, Jane's

Mrs. Westbrook Receives Air Medal For Pilot-Husband Shot Down In Raid

Their Husbands Are Casualties

Three wives received Air Medals at Des Moines Sunday on behalf of their husbands, casualties in the European war area. Left to right they are; Mrs. Roy E. Richards, 3005 Center st., Des Moines; Mrs. Edward S. Stone, Oskaloosa; and Mrs. Hartley A. Westbrook, Coon Rapids; and Maj. Wayne L. Wade, commanding officer of the 345th college training detachment, who presented the medals.

R & T Engraving

Mrs. Hartley A. Westbrook, a teacher in the Coon Rapids public schools, was one of three young wives to receive Air Medals for their hero husbands in a colorful ceremony at the parade grounds at Drake University at Des Moines Sunday.

Maj. Wayne L. Wade, commanding officer of the 345th college training detachment at Drake university, presented the awards on the college parade ground.

The trio of Iowa air lieutenants, casualties of the war, had been cited for "meritorious achievement on bomber combat mission over enemy - occupied continental Europe."

The recipients were:

Mrs. Hartley A. Westbrook, Coon Rapids, whose husband was shot down over Germany May 14 and is now a prisoner of the German government. Lieutenant Westbrook's award had the Oak Leak Cluster, signifying a second Air Medal.

Mrs. Roy E. Richards, 3005 Center st., Des Moines, whose husband was reported missing in action over Lorient, France, on May 17.

Mrs. Edward S. Stone, Oskaloosa, Iowa, whose husband has been missing since Aug. 15 in the European area.

Westbrook is 24; the other two airmen are 25.

The young women, each carrying a sheaf of autumn chrysanthemums in yellow or white, stood before the colors, softly rippling in the breeze, as Major Wade made the presentation.

Included in the group were Mr. and Mrs. B. H. Westbrook, Letts, parents of Lt. Westbrook; Mr. and Mrs. Alva Wagner, Richland, his grandparents; Mr. and Mrs. E. E. Bower, Coon Rapids, Mrs. Westbrook's parents; Mr. and Mrs. E. H. Stone, 2828 Allison ave., Lt. Stone's parents; and Mr. and Mrs. R. W. Squier and Miss Margaret Squier, 3005 Center st, parents and sister of Mrs. Richards.

The Coon Rapids Enterprise account of Jane Westbrook and two other Air Force wives receiving medals at the Drake Parade Grounds (Clipping from the Coon Rapids Enterprise).

7⁵ PM
E.W.T.

JUN 15 1943

VIA SHORT WAVE

Donald Shea
512 E. 41st STREET
BALTIMORE ZONE 18, MD.

Mrs Hartley Westbrook

Letts Iowa

Dear Mrs Westbrook;

        GERMANY ANNOUNNCED THE CAPTURE OF LEUT' HARTLEY WESTBROOK...
There was no messages with the announcment................

Inclosed find application for yourself and family, upon the return
reciept of the application Your name will be placed upon the urgent
list in the event a message should come thru for you from Mr Westbrook,

                Thanking you in advance for your kind
                            Consideration.

            Sincerely ever at your service....

                Donald Shea

Letter from the American Prisoners of War League offering to forward information about Hap as it be came available.

sister. The War Department was most interested in boosting morale, and encouraging interest in the national war effort and public recognition of several of Iowa's young men. Westbrook, one of the first bomber pilots overseas, was one of the first pilots from Iowa to become a Prisoner of War in Europe.

Two other pilots' wives, Mrs. Edward Stone of Oskaloosa, and Mrs. Roy Richards of Des Moines, were also in attendance to receive medal presentations. Their pilot husbands were reported missing in action.

On Sunday afternoon, October 31st, they went to the parade

ground of the 345th College Detachment of the Air Corp at Drake University, Des Moines. On an outdoor stage decorated with flags and bunting, at 1:00 p.m. Rev. Marvin O. Sansbury, of the University Church of Christ, delivered a short address. Major Wayne Wade, who was in charge of the program, read the individual citations, then called the three ladies to the stage and presented their husband's decorations. Jane was awarded Hap's medals, which were a Purple Heart, and the Air Medal with Two Oak Leaf Clusters.

Jane Westbrook is presented Hap's medals by Major Wade and a ceremony held October 31st, 1943, at Drake University drill field.

Since Hap had previously received the Air Medal, Major Wade read the following citation:

"Meritorious Service. For exceptionally meritorious service while participating in five separate bomber combat missions over enemy-occupied Continental Europe. The courage, coolness, and skill displayed by these officers and enlisted men upon these occasions were of the highest order, and reflect great credit upon themselves and the Air Forces of the United States." By Command of Major General Acre.

The Drake Air Cadets marched and the band played several military tunes.

After lunch at a local restaurant, they returned home filled with pride, but concealed their apprehension.

One of the first persons Jane heard from was Lady Dorothy

Jane's parents, Mr. and Mrs. Bowers, and Hap's parents, Mr. and Mrs. Westbrook at the presentation of medals to Jane by Major Wade. (Photo: The Des Moines Register)

Bradley of East Bradenham, Thetford, Norfolk, who had learned of Hap's demise. Lady Bradley was most supportive, writing several letters describing her gardening activities and strawberry preserves. She never mentioned the war or Hap's situation, but addressed everyday activities as life continued in an orderly fashion. She had experienced several years of the war and steeled herself against anticipating the worst.

Jane continued to teach school in the Bayard School system. Teaching school gave her access to gas rationing coupons so she could occasionally visit Hap's parents to share the few letters that survived censorship. Making lesson plans and grading papers were isolated work, and did not expose her to the daily contact with people in the retail store who asked a variety of personal questions, reminding her of Hap's absence. She appreciated the privacy, not having to answer questions from a community who wanted to share her concerns. Working with the young children helped to focus Jane's attention, and take comfort in their world, free of fear.

LETTER FROM HAP TO JANE AND FAMILY: KRIEGSGEFANGENENENPOST, MIT LUFTPOST PAR AVION

GEPROUIT/22   U.S. CENSOR/EXAMINED by 292
Dulag Luft   Deutschland (Allemagne)

An: Mrs. Hartley A Westbrook
Emphangsort: Coon Rapids
StraBe: Iowa
Land: USA

Dear Jane & Mom & Dad. May 19, 1943
You are probably worried but I am OK. I bailed out over water near Keil, Germany and not injured. May 13. I am a prisoner of war deep in the heart of Germany XXXXXX. I am feeling good and will do everything possible to keep fit and well. For cigarettes ask the Red Cross, they'll tell you what to do and what to send. I am able to take care of myself and look out for myself, now until the wars over, then my wife will, now as far as I am concerned. All we need to think about now is our own home and what we'll do. I guess my flying is over for now and sometime. I know you'll send what you can (candy & Cigs) and your love & letters is all that doesn't worry me. Just remember I am allright and don't worry and "Hap" will look out for his self. My crew are most all safe, and opposition was great although I did my best. You will write all necessary relatives for me and keep on looking after our affairs and keep your chin up ole' girl I'll be back. I can only write two of these a month but I am expecting lots from you. Please say hello to all for me, I know you will, and do write. I am constantly thinking of you and I got to keep my ring that you sent me as a wedding ring and as long as I live I'll wear it. With all my Love & Kisses
Hartley

Hartley Westbrook's first letter home after being taken as a prisoner of war, six days after being shot down. Subjects were limited, and the letter is guarded about a number of things.

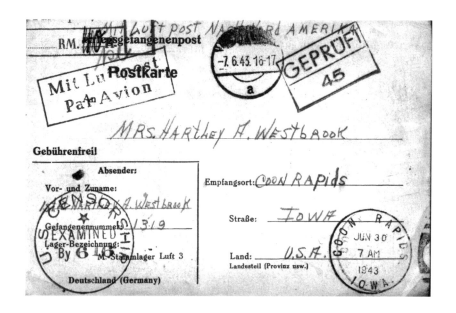

Kriegsgefangenenlager

Datum: MAY 29 1943

Darling: now thats the shocks over I haunt the mail for something that only you write and please say things as we would if I were there for the days grow nearer there are six of us in a room and we bitch like on a fishing trip. I am resting up and feel great. I'll be a grand dad soon if I dont get a razer but I guess being a father comes first but whats the diff I still can be one of those too Love Hartley

Kriegsgefangenenlager   Datum: Oct 23, 1944

Dear Grandpa's: Jane says you asked her my plans, which arn't very definite yet, so you know I must start thinking about my post war plans. You know of what I am referring to? If I cant get what I want for the job I want, well then I'll have to go back to school and try to find something else or stay in the army I'll have to have a job. Hartley

Kriegsgefangenenlager   Datum: Nov 30, 1944

Dear Grandpa's: As I sit and watch a fall moon come up and enjoy the freshness and crispness of the air I hope you are enjoying the same. I am chilly at times an other than that I feel good and expect to be home again soon. Mail is quite slow. As Ever Hartley

WAR DEPARTMENT
Army Service Forces
~~SERVICES OF SUPPLY~~

OFFICE OF THE ADJUTANT GENERAL
AG 201 Westbrook, Hartley A.   WASHINGTON
(22 Sept 43)PD-C AS#O-728,041   22 September 1943.

Mrs. Hartley A. Westbrook,

Coon Rapids, Iowa.

My dear Mrs. Westbrook:

I have the honor to inform you that by direction of the
President, the Air Medal has been awarded to your husband, First
Lieutenant (then Second Lieutenant) Hartley A. Westbrook, Air
Corps, for exceptionally meritorious achievement. In addition to
the Air Medal an Oak-leaf Cluster, which indicates the second
award of the same decoration, has been awarded to your husband,
while serving as First Lieutenant.

Since your husband has been reported to the War Department
as a prisoner of war of the German Government, the decoration
will be presented to you in his absence. The decoration will be
forwarded through the Commanding General, Seventh Service Command,
Omaha, Nebraska, to an officer of a nearby Air Corps installation
for presentation to you. The officer selected to make the presentation will communicate with you concerning your wishes in the
matter.

May I again express my sympathy during this period and join
you in the hope for your husband's safe return as quickly as
possible.

Sincerely yours,

H. B. LEWIS,
Brigadier General,
Acting The Adjutant General.

*In September of 1943, Jane received a letter informing her of the medals Hap had
received, and making arrangements for a presentation ceremony.*

CHAPTER TEN
STALAG LUFT III

Stalag Luft III was opened in April 1942 and was built in the middle of a remote forested area by Russian prisoners. There were two adjoining camps, one housing Russians and Polish prisoners and the other housing English and Canadian airmen. The base contained thirty or so barracks, approximately 175 feet by 50 feet, built off the ground about thirty inches. There was an area for activities and ball games, and for the numerous roll calls, or appels, to count prisoners. The addition of captured airmen meant construction of additional compounds of like design.

The camp was surrounded by two twelve feet high barbed wire fences, spaced about five feet apart. Between the fences was barbed wire entanglements filling the area. Another single wire inside the fences twelve feet, mounted about thirty inches high, identified a no-trespass area. Two high voltage wires were mounted on the inside fence. At the corners and every 150 yards, there was an imposing twenty-five foot high tower on which were mounted machine guns and a spotlight, and were manned twenty-four hours per day. The American, British and Russian compounds were also separated by dual barbed wire fencing spaced about fifteen feet apart. There were no entanglements in this area, and it provided a space where Americans and Brits could occasionally mingle.

The barracks were uniformly spaced fifteen to twenty feet apart, and were patrolled at night by German soldiers and German police dogs, turned loose to roam the area.

The barracks were wooden prefabricated buildings, lifted off the ground about two and one-half feet on pilasters of brick. Exterior walls were wooden studs covered with three-quarter inch boards. The interior walls were studs covered with plywood, and doors were of barn door construction. The barracks were divided into eight-man rooms with a central corridor. One end of the barracks contained four-person rooms for commanding officers, and the opposite end contained a latrine, or abort, consisting of a concrete tank with holes cut in it. Lavatories consisted of a long concrete trough with faucets in some units and porcelain sinks in other units.

There were no showers. The prisoners improvised a shower by punching holes in a metal bucket, and showered by pouring another bucket of cold water into it. Prisoners were lucky to schedule a shower every three or four weeks. A year or so later a shower building was built outside the compound, and prisoners, were permitted a semi-warm shower once a month, a privilege denied for insubordination.

Upon entering the camp, the first task after assignment of barracks quarters was to pick up a mattress and pillow ticking and proceed to a large stack of straw. The mattress sack and pillow were stuffed with the fresh straw, and would last as long as they were in camp. The odor of straw was familiar to Hap, since he had been involved in threshing on the farm and brought back memories of home. Those memories were short lived, since in a week the straw was reduced to dusty toothpicks. Attempts to fluff the straw only made matters worse, and one had to adapt to the lumpy uncomfortable bag of straw. The pillow was even worse, since the thin fabric was penetrated by the sharp, coarse straw.

As the war continued, new prisoners arrived each week, and before long, the eight-man rooms held twelve persons with bunks stacked three high. Four bunk stands, a table and small metal heating stove crowded the available space. Each prisoner was given one "brick" of coal per week during winter for heating the space. It was also used for cooking when foodstuffs were available. Each room had French casement windows that swung out, and wood shutters to cover the windows that were closed at night for security.

The base also contained a building with individual cells for solitary confinement. A cook shack was used to prepare the kriegie soup. Outside the fences were housing and offices for the prison guards and staff.

As the number of prisoners increased the camp expanded three times, and prisoners were separated by nationality. The Germans attempted to never have more than 2,000 prisoners in any one camp, but as the war progressed the camp expanded to four camps with 11,000 officers: 6,000 Americans and 5,000 British. The Russian and Polish officers were in the East compound, the Brits and Canadians in the North compound, and Americans in the South compound. Occasionally, the Brits and Americans were able to mingle, which was instrumental in several escape attempts.

The grounds were bare earth, and originally contained tree stumps every four or five feet from clearing the forest. After the first winter the stumps had been dug out and burned for warmth, leaving barren sandy soil. During the rainy season the assembly area turned to mud, and constant appels made conditions most unpleasant.

German soldiers were called "goons" by the prisoners, named after "Alice, the Goon Girl", a particularly unattractive character found in the popular "Popeye" comic strips of the thirties. When the Germans asked what "goons" stood for, the prisoners explained that it was an acronym for 'German Officers and Non-Commissioned Officers,' which seemed to satisfy the guards.

The Germans also had specially trained soldiers who mingled with the prisoners, trying to pick up any information about escape activities, or useful tidbits. They were called "ferrets" and lived up to their moniker. The ferrets spoke English and understood American slang with all of its subtleties. One or two ferrets were sympathetic to the prisoners, and responded to bribes whenever a camera or special item was needed. But most ferrets followed the party line and were cooperative only to unsuspectingly gain information.

As the special language of the prisoners developed, they referred to themselves as "kriegies", a diminutive of Kriegsgefangener. Escape was on everyone's mind, and this constant consideration gave the kriegies hope and helped to maintain sanity. The Americans were very supportive of one another, helping each other in personal distress and/or depression. It was noted that the English, however, maintained a social and cultural hierarchy that reflected their "position" in their home country.

For the young airmen, ages 19 to 25, their first concern was survival, supporting one another to live through this ordeal and returning home to their loved ones. They had lived through a serious depression, having to do without many things, but it would not begin to approach the tribulations facing them during their prison experience. Their second concern was escape.

As a military organization, the officers continued to function as in a military manner. Military protocol was observed, and the men were encouraged to keep clean, close shaven, shoes cleaned and clothes neat. It was difficult without basic materials and tools at hand, but the effort was made, and it helped to maintain morale. The American military organization of the camp consisted of:

S1 - Personnel
S2 - Intelligence (and counter-intelligence)
S3 - Operations
S4 - Supply

Intelligence established a Commander X whose responsibility was to coordinate all escape attempts, making certain one attempt did not expose another major planned escape. It was a delicate situation, demanding the utmost secrecy, and the many escape and intelligence activities were never compromised by the several thousand POWs.

Hap Westbrook was a part of the leadership team, and served on the interrogation committee that interviewed all incoming prisoners. Since the prisoners came from all walks of life, they were interviewed to see what they could contribute to the "community" organization. There were bakers, printers, pickpockets, bankers, mining engineers, leather workers, toolmakers, farmers, electrical engineers, forgers, carpenters, and every trade imaginable.

This was important for several reasons. It helped to maintain the meager supplies and clothing, but also helped to establish teams for breaking out of camp. The forgers created passports, German identification and working papers, printed Deutchmarks, and documents that might be used in an escape. Tailors not only kept kriegie uniforms in repair, but actually made copies of German soldiers uniforms. Dyes were made to match uniform and civilian clothes that were to be used in a breakout. Prisoners purloined pieces of metal to make scissors for cutting hair, and nippers and pliers for cutting barbed wire. The prisoners also managed to steal enough parts to assemble a receiving radio and a transmitting radio. The assembled talents were amazing.

The prisoner leadership team was particularly careful to screen German "inserts" posing as downed airmen. German counter-intelligence attempted a number of devices to gain inside information on the planning and activities of the prisoners.

CHAPTER ELEVEN
KRIEGSBROT AND SOUP

The German Camp Commandant was Oburst Friedrich-Wilhelm Von Lindeiner who had fought in WW I, had been wounded several times, and won the Iron Cross. In the late thirties, he accepted an appointment in the Luftwaffe as a member of the personal staff of Field Marshall Herman Goering. The commandant, in his sixties, was appointed camp commandant in 1942. His deputy was Major Gustov Simoleit, a college professor who spoke five languages fluently.

Colonel Von Lindeiner insisted upon strict compliance with Geneva Accords. He was relieved from command after the "Great Escape". He was not shot as the movie showed but confined for 12 months in camp. He died May 22, 1963, at the age of 82.

Von Lindeiner had a most difficult task. The German High Command sent numerous rules and regulations that were almost impossible to carry out. There was conflict between the Gestapo Police and the Luftwaffe Prison Command. It was complicated by the High Command's position to shoot first and ask questions later.

One visiting German officer's job was to update the prisoners on the progress of the war. Of course the Germans were "always winning" and he would usually announce, "Gentlemen, you are helpless and hopeless. When Germany wins the war, you will stay here to help build Germany." He did not realize that the young airmen would have choice words for him, but they held their tongues for fear of reprisal.

The Commandant pled with the leaders of the recalcitrant young captives to refrain from their incessant escape attempts because it reflected on his performance as a commander. He was held to a high standard of performance, and any successful escape would lead to his court-martial or even execution. As it turned out, after a major escape he was relieved of command, and as he left the compound under guard, commented to the American Commander, "You will be in Berlin before I will."

The German Camp Organization consisted of:

Group 1. Commandant and court officer
Group 2. Administration of the various compounds
Group 3. Counterintelligence
Group 4. Administration
Group 5. Medical branch
Group 6. Mail and censorship
Group 7. Guards
Group 8. Military officer of the barracks

There were over eight hundred staff and guards at the Stalag, most of them over age or non-combatants. The prisoners tried to keep the guards busy so as to not release any of the guards for active service combat.

The Germans were fully cognizant of the Geneva Convention for the treatment of prisoners, and conscientiously attempted to fulfill their obligations. As the war dragged on it was more difficult to meet Geneva conditions, because delivery of food and care packages was interrupted by Allied bombing and strafing of railroads and highways.

As previously noted, the two most important things on a kriegie's mind were freedom and food. The prisoners were served one meal a day. That

Photograph taken by the Germans after being processed as a prisoner of war May 13th, 1943.

An Iowa Pilot Named Hap

meal consisted of a very watery soup and a crust of black bread called Kriegsbrot. The POWs suspected that instead of flour, sawdust was the main ingredient in the bread.

Westbrook's first trip through the food line made a lasting impression. When he received his cup of watery soup, certain unidentified objects in the soup were wiggling, and he refused to eat for three days. On the fourth day, hunger pangs gave way, and he closed his eyes and wolfed down his soup and bread.

The POWs would not have survived if it were not for the International Red Cross who furnished each prisoner a food parcel every week. Each package provided: dried fruit, biscuit, powdered milk, soup powder, bouillon powder, several sugar cubes, instant coffee, can of Spam, can of ham and eggs, small brick of cheese, small can of liver paste, small tin of butter, vitamin c tablets, orange concentrate, a small concentrated chocolate bar and six packs of cigarettes. The contents were selected for diet, but the quantity of food would barely sustain low-level hunger pangs for a person for a week.

POWs would prepare meals on their room stoves, and created some interesting concoctions to share with their fellow kriegies. Each prisoner stored a small cache of food, in case emergency circumstances required it. Cigarettes were a coveted trading item, between prisoners and guards and between each other.

All prisoners would trade what they did not currently need for items that were in great need at some particular time. Westbrook, while 'horse-trading' cigarettes within the compound, was owed over $1,400 by other prisoners. When they were released from the German prison he forgave all debts.

Packages from home were a welcome addition, and were inspected several times by the Germans to assure no weapons were being smuggled into the enclosure. Since the Germans were also experiencing difficult times, items were often taken from the parcels. Cakes rarely made it through inspections, but cookies usually did, and were shared with the roommates. Soap, toothpaste and socks were the most coveted items received from home. The delivery of packages was erratic, sometimes taking six months or more.

Every three months, the German Command would have an

official inspection of the premises, with several ranking officers inspecting every building. On one such inspection a German colonel had a beautiful German shepherd dog in tow. The dog was given to an aide to escort through the barracks, and the aide gave it to an accompanying POW to escort through the buildings. When the inspecting group was about two-thirds through the inspection, the dog was missing. The staff retraced their steps, and the animal could not be found. Nor could traces of hair, dog collar or remains. One can only assume that the protein intake of the next meal in the camp increased by approximately sixty pounds.

GNEIXENDORF
TEILLAGER DER LUFTWAFFE
LAGERFÜHRUNG

CAMP REGULATIONS

JAN. 1, 1944

1 EVERY GERMAN OFFICER MUST BE SALUTED. WHEN SALUTING, HANDS OUT OF POCKETS, CIGARETTES AND PIPES OUT OF MOUTH.
2 ALL GERMAN SOLDIERS IN CHARGE OF ADMINISTRATIVE OR GUARD FUNCTIONS (INCLUDING AUXILARY GUARDS EITHER IN UNIFORM OR IN CIVIL CLOTHES WITH ARMBANDS) AND ALL ARMED FORCE OFFICIALS, IF ON DUTY, ARE SUPERIORS TO THE PRISONERS OF WAR. THEIR ORDERS HAVE TO BE EXECUTED UNCONDITIONALLY AND IMMEDIATELY.
3 ROLL CALL IS MILITARY DUTY! SO BLOUSE AND OVERCOAT BUTTONED, MILITARY (NOT CIVIL) CAP AND SHOES!
4 EVERYONE WHO AT SIGNAL FOR ROLL CALL, DOES NOT FALL OUT IMMEDIATELY AND DIRECTLY SHOWS DISREGARD TO WARDS HIS COMRADES ALREADY STANDING ROLL CALL.
5 ONLY THOSE HAVING A SPECIAL WRITTEN PERMIT FOR A SPECIFIED TIME FROM THE DOCTOR ARE ALLOWED IN THE BARRACKS DURING ROLL CALL.
6 WHILE ON PARADE KEEP QUIET, AND OBSERVE MILITARY DISCIPLINE (NO SHOUTING, SMOKING NOR PLAYING)!
7 AFTER ROLL CALL LEAVE IN FULL ORDER. (NO RUNNING FROM PARADE GROUND).
8 ALL PRISONERS OF WAR, EXCEPT DISABLE, HAVE TO CARRY OUT ORDERS CONCERNING THEIR OWN BENEFIT. THOSE REFUSING TO WORK WILL BE FORCED TO
9 CHOW DETAIL. WHEN WHISTLED OUT, HAVE TO FALL OUT IMMEDIATELY.
10 EVERYBODY TO BE DELIVERED INTO INFIRMARY, ISOLATION OR HOSPITAL, AS WELL AS SUCH DETACHED TO SPECIAL WORKS OR SERVICES HAVE TO GIVE THEIR NAMES, SECOND NAMES AND NUMBERS TO THEIR BARRACK CHIEF WHO HAS TO INFORM THE RESPECTIVE GERMAN COMPANY CHIEF.
11 PRISONERS OF WAR IN ISOLATION ARE NOT ALLOWED TO PAY VISITS OUTSIDE OF ISOLATION NOR TO RECEIVE VISITORS NOT ISOLATE
12 THOSE TOUCHING WARNING WIRE OR ENTERING AREA WARNED NOT TO WILL BE FIRED ON WITHOUT WARNING.
13 HANGING UP LAUNDRY, BLANKETS, ETC. ON ANY BARRED WIRE IS STRICTLY PROHIBITED. HANG THEM ON THE STAKES DESTINED FOR THIS PURPOSE.
14 MISPLACING DOG-TAGS HAS TO BE REPORTED AT ONCE.
15 PRISONERS OF WAR WHO HAVE TO LEAVE CAMP FOR ANY REASON (E.G. FOR HOSPITAL; DELOUSING; WORKS OUTSIDE OF CAMP SUCH UNLOADING RED CROSS PARCELS) ARE NOT ALLOWED MORE THAN ONE PACKAGE OF CIGARETTE OR TOBACCO. EXCESSIVE QUANTITIES WILL BE CONFISCATED.
16 ADDRESS REQUIREMENTS, WISHES ETC. ONLY TO YOUR BARRACK CHIEF WHO WILL PASS THEM ON TO THE GERMAN COMPANY CHIEF.
17 CONSULTING HOURS FOR GERMAN "COMPANY CHIEFS" ONLY FROM 9-10 AND 15-16 O'CLOCK BY BARRACK CHIEFS ONLY.

OBERST u. KOMMANDANT (GEZ. KUHN)

Hand lettered document defining how the Stalag Luft III is to be regulated. These were regularly issued and rigidly adhered to.

CHAPTER TWELVE
PRISON LIFE

The roll call, or appel, in the prison camp occurred twice daily. All prisoners would line up, and their presence confirmed by the camp staff to assure there had been no escapes. The young officers were not always cooperative, and the opportunity to confuse or harass the staff reached ridiculous proportions. The Germans would respond with strong-arm tactics, threats of punishment, and actual punishment to keep them in line.

The crushing boredom and ennui of prison subjugation was individually humiliating and debilitating. Until denied, freedom is an abstraction, especially to an American who has never known the pain, agony and despair of it being forcefully denied.

At one appel, the POWs were milling around breaking ranks, responding twice to names that were called and being generally uncooperative. The goons dismissed the POWs, and a few minutes later reassembled them. The POWs were called to attention and immediately surrounded by German soldiers armed with machine guns. The soldiers threatened to shoot anyone who moved, talked or answered incorrectly. Needless to say, the POWs complied, at least for the next few appels.

Keeping clothes in repair was a major concern and clothing was patched and re-patched constantly. The prisoners were adept in scrounging materials, or recycling, to keep from becoming a rag-tag group. One young man had a sweater that was in bad repair, so he unraveled it and knitted a pair of socks. When he threw away the old pair of socks, they were immediately snatched up, repaired, and replaced a pair in worse condition.

Shoe repair was non-existent. Westbrook approached the American staff to make a request to the German staff about constructing a small building to house a shoe repair facility. The American staff approved, and the Germans recognized its value and prefabricated a building, drawn to Westbrook's specifications. Tools were manufactured from purloined material. Leather for repairs and thread were furnished by the YMCA, and the repair shop became a big success. The space was large enough that a section

The shoe repair shop built and equipped at Westbrook's suggestion. Hap is shown here with three gentlemen officers learning the cobbler trade. (photo: German Staff)

was set aside for a barbershop. A barber chair was fashioned from a wooden Red Cross packing crate, scissors and a comb were handcrafted, and another new enterprise began to serve the kriegies.

These enterprises were important, because they not only provided much needed service, but they gave the POWs something to do. With all the youth and enthusiasm, nothing to do, and nothing to do it with, the main concern was how to keep mentally and physically occupied to maintain sanity, as well as defeat depression. There were a few disciplinary problems, but Americans tended to look after one another and protect each other, just as they had performed in their planes.

The Young Men's Christian Association (YMCA) was instrumental in providing sports equipment for the prisoners. The regional headquarters for the YMCA was located a few miles from Sagan, and members of the headquarters visited the camp regularly. They furnished games, chessboards, ball gloves and balls, soccer balls and other sports items used to occupy the prisoners' time. They also provided a few band instruments that the prisoners shared. Prisoners made cards from wrapping paper or pasteboard, and bridge games were constantly in progress.

Prisoners regularly walked around inside the prison walls, not

Building the theater was a major undertaking by these POWs. Hap worked with the theater arts people, drew up the plans, and oversaw the construction. It was an enormously successful venture and provided a creative outlet for many of the talented POWs. (photo: German Staff)

only to keep active, but also to keep in shape in case they had an opportunity to escape. Groups would circle the camp, passing on the rumors of the day, discussing opportunities for escape, or repeating messages received from home. It also gave relief from the close quarters in the bunkrooms. It was a daily ritual, rain or shine.

Sometime after the success of the shoe repair shop, some thought was given to building a theater, where plays could be performed. Westbrook was given the assignment of drawing plans and presenting them to the German Staff. The German Command saw the benefits, provided the prisoners with the materials to construct a theater, complete with sloping dirt floor, stage, proscenium arch, orchestra pit, and electric lighting. Several prisoners were playwrights, and others active in stage production. Seating for four hundred persons was again created using Red Cross packing crates. The crates had sloped backs and rounded armrests, and were offset for better visibility. The theater proved to be enormously successful, with many performances of existing and new plays. Sets were built, songs were written with parodies of prison life most raucous. It was used for Sunday services for all faiths. It was a great device to relieve boredom, keep the mind sharp, and morale high.

The building was made large enough to provide space for a small library. Books received from home were added to the library, along with Red Cross contributions, which were a valuable resource for use by all in the camp. German newspapers and camp publications were also later made available.

The theater was so successful, it was recommended by the German Staff to other Stalags as a way to involve the prisoners in creative activity.

Westbrook's enterprising nature and Iowa can-do attitude was a valuable commodity in the prison community.

One event, not initiated by Westbrook, was too successful.

The prisoners received a variety of dried fruit in their Red Cross parcels, and a chemical engineer convinced the prisoners that they should be saved for a special occasion. The engineer found a large container and proceeded to brew fruit wine. After adequate ageing, a still was devised from a trombone borrowed from the prison band, and some very high-octane "kriegie-lightning" was produced in a fair quantity. Since July Fourth was near at hand, they decided to have a special Independence Celebration.

The Brits from the camp next door were invited to the celebration, as they were originally a part of the initial cause for the celebration. Since the prisoners had been on severe rations their resistance to alcohol was nil, and it took only a small amount of the liquid for them to become extremely inebriated. Even some of the goons joined in the celebration, and before long, the entire camp was reeling. At the end of the day, it was impossible to steer the prisoners to their respective barracks. It took several days for prisoners to recover from their hangovers, and to be sorted to their respective assigned locations.

The German Staff acknowledged the therapeutic effect of the break in the routine, but instituted more diligent inspections to ensure it would never happen again.

Escape and harassment were still paramount in the young

airmen's minds. Any device to upset their captors or divert their attention was used. The POWs were creative in their attempts to irritate and confound the goons.

At night, when the camp was closed down and the police dogs turned loose to roam, a kriegie would open a casement window, reach under the shutter, and pound on the side of the building with his hand. The police dogs would immediately rush to the noise, barking furiously. Immediately, several barracks away, another kriegie would repeat the pounding, and the dogs would frantically chase to the new location. After seven or eight times, the dogs would be in a panic. A German soldier, in disgust, would fire a round of ammunition alongside a barracks wall, hoping to catch an extended arm, and the camp would be quiet for the remainder of the night.

When an appel was called, the camp and the German staff assembled in a particular arrangement. In the area where the German command would stand, the kriegies would dig holes about eight inches deep, and cover them with sticks and a thin layer of dirt. The proud Prussians would have to watch their step from stumbling to their assigned positions. This embarrassed the German staff and entertained the kriegies enormously.

Other times, a prisoner would "accidentally" drop a piece of paper in the yard, with an unusual message on it. The ferrets would immediately retrieve it, suspecting a coded message, and spend a good deal of time trying to decipher it. It kept the ferrets busy for hours, and the false message had achieved its goal of disrupting the command routine.

Since the buildings were built on piers, at night ferrets would crawl under the building to listen to conversations, hoping to discover tunneling information or data about an escape plan. Kriegies would respond by spreading broken glass or shards of sharp tin under the building to discourage eavesdropping. One housing group, suspecting an under-floor intruder, heated a pan of water to boiling temperature and poured it through cracks in the floor. The resulting muffled "shist" and the hasty exit from under the floor exposed the would-be spy.

Right, Lt. Col. McNickle, Hauptmann Galathovics, Hohendahl and Embach.

Below, a class in session at "Sagan University."

Above, Fred Loomis kept the Compound watches ticking.

Below, Robert Kemp, W. W. Saunders and librarians.

Photos from Stalag Luft III from a German camp newspaper depicting activities in the prison camp.

CHAPTER THIRTEEN
ESCAPE

There was always talk about escaping and finding a way to the front lines. It consumed the POWs' time, gave them hope, and fueled their desires to return home. And it kept them focused on something positive.

The German Commandant's pleading to refrain from attempting to escape went un-heeded as the young airmen devised plans to exit from the camp.

One attempt involved a shallow excavation, under the wire fencing, using a "mole technique." Under the cover of darkness, two prisoners dug a shallow trench heaping dirt on their backs as they inched forward. The escape activity was spotted by a searchlight, and the prisoners were detected before they were half-way under the fences.

Two young men managed to "requisition" some steel straps and fashioned two wire cutters. Under cover of night while a diversion was created at one end of the camp, the airmen attempted to cut their way through the barbed wire entanglements. Partway through the middle entanglements they were discovered, re-captured, and placed in solitary confinement on kriegsbrot and water for ten days.

Another time the prisoner-made German uniforms were put to use. Kriegies managed to carve wooden rifles and side arms, and color them to look most realistic. The uniforms were accurately tailored, dyed to match German uniform colors, and insignia created to match corresponding rank. Late one afternoon several fake goons marched a group of prisoners toward the exit gates, appearing as a work detail to perform tasks, or take a hot shower, outside the barbed wire enclosure. About thirty prisoners had passed through the gates when a German soldier recognized one of the American airmen dressed as a guard, and immediately sounded the alarm. All the prisoners were rounded up and all placed in solitary confinement on bread and water for ten days.

Often so many prisoners were caught performing punishable acts that there was a waiting list for solitary confinement.

The German Commandant repeatedly pled with the kriegies not to try to escape. As the war became more severe for the Germans, constant threats were made to subdue the desire of the young airmen to gain their freedom. Had the POWs escaped they would have been treated harshly by the German populace who were particularly incensed because of bombing by the Allied "hooligans."

Two young airmen developed a bold plan for escape during daylight hours. They located some lumber, made some nails and built two ladders about fourteen feet long. They induced other POWs to build a boxing ring, with four posts and wire for the ropes. After a series of beginning bouts, a real "grudge match" was created, with threats and shouting. The German guards had watched with amusement at the preliminary matches, but the ensuing fracas really captured their attention. The fight was half wrestling, half boxing, and was furiously contested.

While the match was underway, the two young escapees put a ladder up the first fence, and spanned the two fences with the second ladder. The first young airman dropped to the other side, and as the second airman crossed the ladder bridge, it collapsed, dropping him into the wire entanglements. The guards chased the first escapee for some time, until they captured him. The second escapee was left dangling and screaming until the first was caught. Both were sent to solitary, and the entire camp denied certain privileges for helping the young men with the boxing charade.

The latrine, or abort, was periodically cleaned by a Polish man, dressed in a German uniform, who would visit with his "honey wagon" pulled by oxen, and whose job it was to haul human excrement out of the camp. The prisoners used to tease him, trying to teach him to talk American slang. This enabled them to steal whatever was useful to the prisoners. One day they diverted the attention of the driver, and a young airman crawled into the "honey wagon" to make his escape. He carried a change of clothing and a bar of lye soap to bathe with after getting out of the compound, since the stench was permeating and difficult to get rid of. The success of his attempted escape is unknown, but it was a novel, if disgustingly smelly, attempt at freedom.

To all Prisoners of War!

The escape from prison camps is no longer a sport!

Germany has always kept to the Hague Convention and only punished recaptured prisoners of war with minor disciplinary punishment.

Germany will still maintain these principles of international law.

But England has besides fighting at the front in an honest manner instituted an illegal warfare in non combat zones in the form of gangster commandos, terror bandits and sabotage troops even up to the frontiers of Germany.

They say in a captured secret and confidential English military pamphlet,

THE HANDBOOK OF MODERN IRREGULAR WARFARE:

". . . the days when we could practise the rules of sportsmanship are over. For the time being, every soldier must be a potential gangster and must be prepared to adopt their methods whenever necessary."

"The sphere of operations should always include the enemy's own country, any occupied territory, and in certain circumstances, such neutral countries as he is using as a source of supply."

England has with these instructions opened up a non military form of gangster war!

Germany is determined to safeguard her homeland, and especially her war industry and provisional centres for the fighting fronts. Therefore it has become necessary to create strictly forbidden zones, called death zones, in which all unauthorised trespassers will be immediately shot on sight.

Escaping prisoners of war, entering such death zones, will certainly lose their lives. They are therefore in constant danger of being mistaken for enemy agents or sabotage groups.

Urgent warning is given against making future escapes!

In plain English: Stay in the camp where you will be safe! Breaking out of it is now a damned dangerous act.

The chances of preserving your life are almost nil!

All police and military guards have been given the most strict orders to shoot on sight all suspected persons.

Escaping from prison camps has ceased to be a sport!

An Iowa Pilot Named Hap

CHAPTER FOURTEEN
THE GREAT ESCAPE

The boldest plan for escape was to tunnel out of the encampment. It began when the Americans and the Brits were in the same camp, and was carried out after the Americans were placed in their own camp. It took a good deal of imagination, engineering and patience to attempt such a venture.

Tunneling out of the camp was always a considered option. The tunnels would have to be deep, since goons traversed the camp with a steel rod about six feet long, intermittently probing for tunnels. The British actually dug four tunnels, three as escape routes, and one to be found, to divert the Germans from further inspections. The tunnels were named Tom, Dick and Harry, for security purposes.

In tunnel Harry, access was gained under the stove housing in a barracks close to the fence. The concrete slab supporting the stove was lifted, a hole chopped through the concrete foundation under the building and a shaft dropped about thirty feet. From there they tunneled horizontally as much as one hundred fifty feet. Since the soil was a sandy loam, the ceiling had to be supported, and mattress support boards were taken from bunks for the enclosure. The soil removed was ingeniously distributed around the base. Men cut sleeves out of their shirts, made a string closure at the cuff, filled them with soil and stuffed them down their pants. As the men went for their daily 'walk-abouts', they would pull the string and release the dirt, and scuff it into the other soil. Some POWs started a vegetable garden, and the height of the soil grew daily.

Since the tunneling work was confined, a duct built of Red Cross tins taped together was run the length of the tunnel and a bellows built to force fresh air into the space. The depth of the excavation muffled the sound from electric listening devices. The prisoners found wiring and electric lights for the length of the tunnel. A wooden rail track was devised, and a dolly built to roll through the tunnel rather than having to crawl.

The three thousand men in camp contributed as necessary to provide safety and security. Frequent appels were called, and men had to scramble out of the hole to make roll call, so as not to invite closer inspections.

While the tunnels were being dug, operations had forgers making documents to assist the airmen after their escape. Work papers, identity papers, Deutchmarks and other documents were manufactured. A pinhole camera was made and YMCA film used for taking photos for passports. Official stamps were made from the tops of rubber boots and inkpad colors mixed to match official documents. Tailors made over two hundred suits, shirts and ties in the style of the general German populace. Candidates for escape had to speak German, Polish or French, and classes were set up to improve levels of conversation. The organization, timing and security were successfully maintained in the British camp.

One day when three or four POWs were talking to a goon, a sleeve of dirt one of the prisoners carried was accidentally discharged. The men started an animated discussion, scuffing the dirt. The goon, unaware of the accident, helped scuff the soil, until the prisoners alertly drew him away from the area.

The original plans for the tunnel called for it to exit in the forest, about sixty feet outside the fences. When the mining engineers determined they were within twenty feet of the exit into the trees, final preparations were made for the escape. Two hundred volunteers were prepared to leave, and assembled in the barracks. If you were caught in uniform you were an escaped prisoner, but if caught in civilian clothes you would be immediately shot as a spy.

Westbrook decided not to participate, since he was married and knew the consequences if he were caught.

Well after dark the final twenty feet were completed, only to discover they were still twenty feet short of the forest. Since goons patrolled outside the fence all night long, and spotlights would regularly sweep the area, the escapees were released intermittently and dashed to the forest. After seventy-six POWs had left the tunnel, there was a pause while the German sentry made his rounds. The German sentry stopped to relieve himself and found he was urinating in a large opening in the ground. Shouting an alarm, the escape was exposed, and the POWs fled through the forest.

In a massive manhunt taking two weeks, all but three prisoners were rounded up. The German High Command estimated it took fifty men to track down one escaped prisoner. The High Command decided that fifty was a number to be reconciled. The prisoners were held in a special prison until they were loaded into trucks for a return trip to Stalag Luft III. On the outskirts of the camp the trucks stopped so the prisoners could have a toilet break. The POWs were lined up, and fifty of the men were shot, to accommodate the High Command's orders.

Three prisoners were not caught. One prisoner, Bram Vanderstok, was a Dutch National who escaped from Germany and joined the Royal Air Force and became a POW. He ultimately made his way to England, via Belgium, France, Spain and Gibraltar. He re-joined the RAF, completed the war, returned to Holland and became a medical doctor. He immigrated to the United States where he practiced medicine until retirement.

The second airman, Per Bergsland, posed as a Norwegian Nazi, and made it to a northern seaport where Swedish sailors smuggled him aboard a ship bound for Sweden.

The fate of the third prisoner who was not captured is not known.

The escape attempt was later the basis for a movie made in 1963 called, "The Great Escape." It starred Steve McQueen, James Garner, Charles Bronson, Richard Attenborough and James Coburn.

SCHEMATIC OF THE TUNNEL, "HARRY", FOR THE "GREAT ESCAPE"

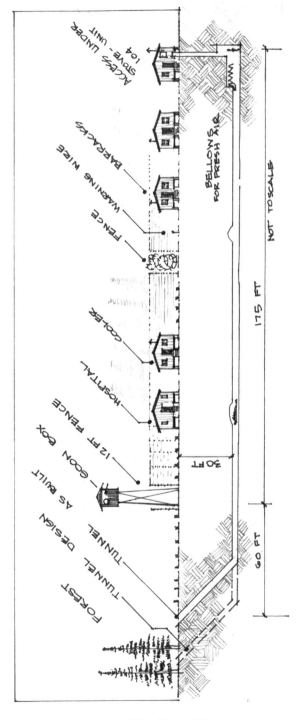

ACCESS UNDER STOVE - UNIT 104

BARRACKS

FENCE WARNING WIRE

COOLER

HOSPITAL

12 FT FENCE

GOON BOX

TUNNEL AS BUILT

TUNNEL DESIGN

FOREST

BELLOWS FOR FRESH AIR

NOT TO SCALE

175 FT

30 FT

60 FT

During the life of the camp, over 100 tunnels were attempted. The three serious ones were "Tom", "Dick" and "Harry". Harry became the main tunnel and the final breakout fell 20' short of the woods. Of the 200 prisoners prepared to leave, only 74 escaped and all but three were recaptured.

An Iowa Pilot Named Hap

CHAPTER FIFTEEN
HOPE

The weather in Sagan consisted of one part Iowa weather and two parts English weather. It was usually cloudy and overcast, much like Britain. During winter months there was snow, freezing temperatures, and an occasional blizzard. Without access to a variety of clothes the prisoners were wet and cold a good deal of the time. The military requirement to keep clean, wash clothes whenever possible, and practice good hygiene reduced sickness substantially.

The YMCA furnished each prisoner with a combination log book/scrapbook. Those with artistic bent filled it with sketches, while others kept a detailed daily diary. Many started with enthusiasm, which trailed off when boredom ensued. Again, an opportunity was offered the prisoners to maintain individuality and exercise latent skills. Hap's logbook is filled with drawings, pictures from home, and pictures taken from German newspapers describing Germany's winning the war, obviously propaganda. It also contains labels from Red Cross supplies and handwritten notes of encouragement from persons working on the cigarette production lines and inserted in cigarette packs. Most prisoners carried their logbook on the long march from prison to prison, and still have them today.

Practically all of the logbooks contained poems written by the young airmen. The poetry topics were very broad and most were philosophical rather than graphic. The quantity and quality of the poetry is an interesting reflection on high school education during the 1920s and 1930s.

One of the young officers had received a package from home that contained a new 78 RPM record, entitled "Pistol Packin' Mama" and it was played on one of several Victrolas which were furnished by the Germans. The tune and words were catchy. "Drinking beer in a cabaret, and was I having fun. Until one night she shot out the light, and now I'm on the run. Oh, lay that pistol down, babe. Lay that pistol down. Pistol packin' mama, lay that pistol down!"

It was a surprise that the tune was not well received by the

POWs. Persons living behind barbed wire found it hard to find much humor in anything other than harassing the Germans.

The Germans permitted setting up a photo processing dark room, and the Red Cross and YMCA managed to furnish small quantities of film. Hap's logbook contains several pictures taken while in Stalag Luft III.

Because of the attempted prisoner tunnel escape, the German Commandant was relieved of his responsibilities, removed from camp in dishonor, and served with a court martial. The new commandant, Colonel Braune, was far more strict, and called for appels several times per day and often in the middle of the night. The unconscionable Gestapo, the secret police, assumed control of the camp relieving the Luftwaffe. Prisoners were informed that any more attempts at escape would end in their being shot. Privileges such as electric lights, use of the library, water, and access to the theater, were intermittently curtailed to keep the kriegies in line.

Electrical engineers in the camp assembled several radios for listening to the broadcast news, and also for transmitting messages to the Allies. The radios were dismantled for storage, so if part of a radio was discovered by the goons a whole new radio did not have to be assembled. Some parts were stored in hollowed table legs in certain barracks, and other parts in a removable panel above the door. The POWs managed to conceal the possession of radios from their captors. Evening radio gathering in a kriegie's room would be secured by an elaborate lookout system that would allow time for dismantling a radio should a ferret drop by. Late in the war listening to the BBC, the young airmen were heartened by the successes of the Allied armies, and started counting the days until they would be released.

As the winter of 1944 approached, the continuing weather was overcast and gray, and snow came early. The prisoners were losing whatever enthusiasm they felt due to the continuing boredom and the repetitious routine of being subjected to the prison schedule. The "great escape" and ultimate result severely affected their attitude and will. As the population of the prison overflowed, there was a total lack of privacy. The fuel allotment was cut back and food provisions were limited to one day's supply inside the prison.

Mail was delivered sporadically. Red Cross packages were less frequent, and the diminished food supplies stretched even further. Many of the newer prisoners had a different mindset, a different attitude, and had difficulty accepting the camp and military discipline. The new prisoners' petulance disrupted the togetherness and discipline that had up to then successfully contributed to prisoner survival. After a short period of time, the new prisoners were made to realize they were "guests" of the German government. Their insolence was not tolerated by either the German staff or the prisoners' military organization.

One young soldier, Ewell Ross McCright, became quite depressed by news from home early in his incarceration. The American commander, Lt. Col. A. P. Clarke, gave him a new responsibility that helped to save his sanity and probably his life. The young officer was given the task of interviewing each prisoner, and building a log of everyone in camp. The information included: name, rank, serial number, assignment, home town, mission when shot down, prison camps, injury record, married status, and some experiences when shot down. This would have been valuable information for the Germans to obtain, but he managed to keep the logbook concealed. When the forced march moved them out of Stalag Luft III, the data was carried by other prisoners and preserved. In 1993, Arnold Wright published "Behind The Wire, Stalag Luft III, South Compound." The book gives a brief history of the logbook, lists all of the prisoners, and is an amazing document. The fact that it was never discovered during the intense inspections after the great escape is truly remarkable.

349. BROWN, ROBERT T 1LT. 0727162 USAAF 138/9 PILOT
R 2 BOX 240   B-24
NORWALK, CALIF.   1306   5-14-43
DULAG LUFT 5-16 TO 5-20 STALAG LUFT III 5-22-43
SHOT DOWN BY FW190'S. BAILED OUT -LANDED IN
ENLEFORD FIORD, GER. PICKED UP IMM BY GER. FISHERMEN.
DOCKS, KIEL, GERMANY
AIR MEDAL 2CL.- SINGLE- P- 3-11-18   21   A

350. EDER, JOHN C 1LT. 0789380   USAAF 125/9 PILOT
114 207TH ST.   B-17
ST. ALBANS, N.Y.   1308   4-14-43
DULAG LUFT 5-17 TO 5-20 STALAG LUFT III 5-22-43.
SHOT DOWN BY FLAK- FW109'S. BAILED OUT -LANDED 7M N.
KEIL, GER. CAPT IMM.
SHIP YARDS, KIEL, GERMANY.
MARRIED- C- 31-3-16   2   O

351. WESTBROOK, HARTLEY A 1LT. 0728041 USAAF 127/7 PILOT
LETTS, IOWA   1319 B-24 5-24-43
DULAG LUFT 5-16 TO 5-20 STALAG LUFT III 5-22-43
SHOT DOWN BY FW190'S. BAILED OUT -LANDED IN BALTIC SEA
10M N. E. KIEL, GER.   PICKED UP IMM BY DANISH
FISHERMEN. GUNSHOT WOUND IN ARM. FLAK IN LEG AND SIDE.
DOCKS, KIEL, GERMANY.
AIR MEDAL 1CL.-MARRIED- P- 29-1-19   1   O

352. SHIEFELBUSH, RICHARD 2LT. 0663417 USAAF 133/9 NAVIGATOR
OSAWATOMIE, KANSAS   1315   B-24 5-14-43
DULAG LUFT 5-16 TO 5-10 STALAG LUFT III 5-22-43
SHOT DOWN BY FW190'S- ME109'S. BAILED OUT -LANDED 10M
N. E. KIEL, GER. PICKED UP BY GER. FISHERMEN.
ACN 245   DOCKS, KIEL, GERMANY.
MARRIED-P- 23-7-18   4   O

353. KLUEVER, LESTER L 1LT 0663385 USAAF 138/12 NAVIGATOR
ATLANTIC, IOWA   1311 B-17 5-14-43
DULAG LUFT 5-16 TO 5-20 STALAG LUFT III 5-22-43.
SHOT DOWN BY FLAK- FIGHTERS. BAILEDOUT -LANDED 10M N.
KIEL. CAPT IMM. SLIGHTLY INJURED BY SHRAPNEL.
ACN 001   SUB. PENS, KIEL, GERMANY
SINGLE-P- 29-2-20   1   AB

354. BISHOP, ROBERT H CAPT. 0353495 USAAF 137/18 NAVIGATOR
913 21 ST   B-24
KNOXVILLE, TENN.   1304   5-14-43
DULAG LUFT 5-16 TO 5-20 STALAG LUFT III 5-22-43
SHOT DOWN BY FW190- ME109'S. BAILED OUT-LANDED 10M N.
KIEL, GER.   PICKED UP BY DANISH FISHERMEN.   MINOR
SHRAPNEL WOUNDS.
DOCKS-SHIPPING YARDS, KIEL, GERMANY.
AIR MEDAL 1 CLU.-SINGLE -P- 16-8-15   19   O

Entries from Wright's book of P.O.W. Ewell McCright's records. How the information was concealed from the Germans is amazing. Westbrook later received a letter from a member of the crew of the Swedish fishing boat that retrieved him from the Baltic Sea.

CHAPTER SIXTEEN
FORCED MARCH

In January 1945, the winter continued to be cold and bitter. Word was received that the Russian Army was advancing and distant cannon fire could be heard in camp. The High Command decided to relocate the prisoners. The German Commander notified the prisoners to start setting aside some food in case the camp would be suddenly evacuated. Late in the evening of January 27th, 1945, the Germans sounded an appel over the public address system. The prisoners dressed, fell into ranks, and were informed the camp was to be evacuated within one hour by foot march. The winter weather had turned nasty, with fifteen-degree temperatures, snow and icy winds. The prisoners hurriedly packed as best they could, selecting what they could wear and what they could carry. Some managed to pick up a Red Cross food parcel, but most had their pockets filled with canned biscuits and ersatz chocolate bars.

Hap was fortunate enough to have his leather flying jacket, and during the summer, had bartered cigarettes for a trench coat. He was wearing his only shoes, the officer's oxfords that Jane had forwarded when he was first in camp. They would prove to be poor hiking shoes in the deep snow and slush.

The snow was over a foot deep when the prisoners passed through the gates into the face of the storm. During this brutal blizzard march lasting six days, they marched sixty-two miles. Every two hours they would stop for a toilet break, and the men would fall onto the snow, exhausted and oblivious to the temperatures and drifts. The second day the Germans passed out a slice of kriegsbrot, and soldiers in the front of the line took only one crust, to ensure that soldiers in the back of the line would get bread. At Freiwaldau they got a few hours of shelter in concentration camp buildings. After four hours rest, they were once again marching into the wind. During one break soldiers searched a farmyard, and in the middle of a haystack found frozen potatoes. One lucky group found a pile of turnip-like vegetables, probably kohlrabi, which were distributed as far as they would go, and the raw vegetables were immediately devoured.

The prisoners were being escorted by teenage cadets from a naval school in their first official action. The cadets brazenly prodded the prisoners along with their bayonets, and the prisoners were too weak and cold to fight back. Eventually the cadets succumbed to the freezing conditions and general misery, and stumbled alongside the prison column, wading through the drifts. It was probably the young cadets first experience in being cold, exhausted and hungry.

Because of the deep snow and the low cut oxfords, Hap experienced some frostbite, and his right foot started to swell up. Walking became impossible for him, but he could not stop since stragglers were being shot. At one farmstead during a stop, Hap found a piece of roofing tin and a length of twine, and fashioned a small sled. Throwing his arm over a fellow prisoner, Hap managed to slide the painful foot along, reducing the pressure and the pain.

Occasionally a prisoner, in desperation, would attempt to make a break for freedom, only to be shot and left to die along the roadside. The guards were small in number and had to attend to the column of prisoners. The ratio of prisoners to guards would have permitted the prisoners to overcome the guards, but there was no advantage. The prisoners did not know their destination, food supply, or what lay ahead. Once in a while, the prisoners would overtake German citizens along the road with their life's possessions loaded on a cart, attempting to find shelter in another community. They, too, were miserable, cold and without food.

The prisoners finally reached a vacant pottery factory, and found respite for one day from the icy blast. They collected wood and started fires to dry out their clothing and gain a small degree of warmth. They nursed their blisters, rearranged their possessions, and slept on the cold dirt floor as best they could. Hap used the opportunity to lance his foot, discharging liquid, and the foot soon returned to normal size. Prisoners nibbled at their rations, not knowing when the next meal would be available.

After ten or twelve hours the men were again assembled, and the column continued another thirty miles in snow that had turned to slush. They traveled through Graustein to Spremberg, a major railroad about ninety miles from Dresden. At the railhead they

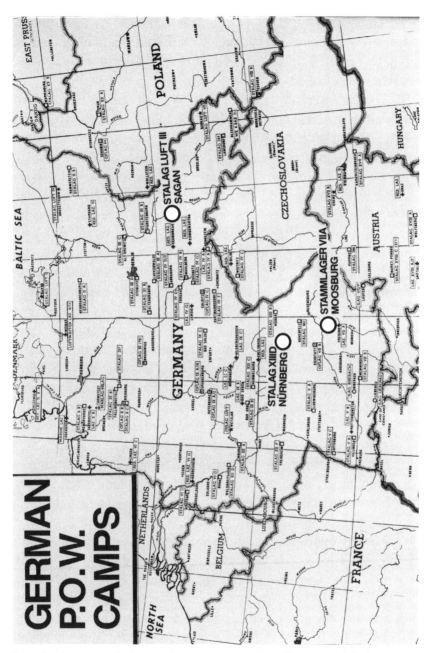

Map showing extent of prisoner of war camps in southern Germany and the location of the forced march from Sagan to Moosburg.

were loaded into rail cars for the two hundred mile trip to Nurnberg. The rail cars were called "40 and 8s" since they held forty men, or eight horses. The prisoners were jammed sixty or seventy to a car, and the doors sealed.

The cars were dirty, uncomfortable, and had no toilet provisions. The men had no reasonable diet, many suffering from diarrhea, and had little control of their bodily functions. In the close air and cold temperatures some prisoners soiled themselves, which only made conditions worse. Occasionally the train would stop for a toilet break, and several thousand men would leave the train, line up with their pants down, relieving themselves. They would again board the train to suffer discomfort, crowding, odors and many indignities to the human condition.

After two days aboard the train they gratefully unloaded in Nurnberg. Some of the prisoners assembled for a march to Stalag XIIID, unaware of the deteriorated and filthy conditions in the camp and the terrors of allied bombing raids. At Nurnberg, prisoners from Stalag Luft III formed ranks and plodded the remaining ninety miles toward Moosburg and Stalag VII. The camp was a mixture of French, Polish, Canadians, English and Americans. Built to hold five thousand prisoners, there were twenty thousand in residence. The camp was best described as a vermin-ridden hellhole.

Allied planes regularly bombed nearby railroad storage yards and military installations. Shrapnel and bomb fragments regularly flew into the prison camp. In order to protect themselves, prisoners dug slit trenches and covered themselves with corrugated tin from damaged buildings. Air raid sirens never seemed to stop.

The prisoners learned that the day the Allied prisoners left Sagan, the Russian prisoners were herded into the forest and shot.

Since the camp was so crowded, prisoners shared beds around the clock. As soon as one prisoner awoke and left his straw ticking, another prisoner moved in, and the process was repeated twenty four hours a day. The remaining prisoners would wander around the camp, sixteen hours a day, close to the outside fence. It was the spring rainy season, and the weather was most disagreeable.

Hap and a friend, Bob Menninga, worked together to stay warm and dry. Each had a blanket, so they would place one blanket on the ground, cover themselves with the other blanket and Hap's trench coat, and found they could stay quite warm. Having hoarded some chocolate bars and biscuits, they nibbled at their cache, since meals were sometimes delivered alternate days.

One day while they were keeping warm next to a building near the fence, Hap and Bob were surprised by a scrawny cat that had wandered into the camp looking for food and affection. In no time at all, the cat was executed, skinned and cleaned. Some scraps of wood were found and a fire started, and the cat cooked on a make-shift spit. It was the first hot meat the two prisoners had eaten in over four months and the first fresh meat since becoming a prisoner.

A greater number of Allied fighter planes were overhead, and the German guards recognized the war had changed and began to abandon the column. The American airmen decided that since the end of their incarceration was near, escape was a futile venture. They became a self-governing organization when they reached the Moosburg Stalag VII. They could have easily over-powered the few guards that were left, but preferred to operate as a camp and maintain discipline until they were liberated.

Because the roads and bridges were regularly bombed and strafed, Germans had a difficult time getting food to the camp and even to their own troops. The Red Cross continued to ship parcels, but delivery was intermittent. The April rains kept the campgrounds in constant mud. The prisoners attempted to clean up the camp and restore some sense of sanitary conditions, but the number of prisoners in the camp made it difficult. The POW commander specifically ordered the men to not attempt to escape, but to maintain group security and await the approaching American Army.

April 28th, 1945, was a gray, foreboding day. There was a good deal of truck noise in the background and plane activity overhead. The prisoners were hoping the roads were being repaired to allow food to be delivered to the camp, since the watery soup could not get any thinner. As the sound of truck traffic grew louder, a tank suddenly appeared on the road through the trees approaching the main gate. Without stopping, the tank crashed through both gates and entered the compound. The lead tank lid popped open and out stepped General George Patton, complete with pearl handled guns.

There was great relief, but not much shouting since the prisoners did not have much energy to make an effusive display. Some men swarmed on the tank, but most expressed relief that their ordeal was near an end. Soon food and medicine would be delivered by the Allies. Mostly, they were appreciative of what it truly meant to be free and relieved from the stress of the unknown.

General Patton's troops were unrelenting in pursuing the enemy. A few days before, they had passed through Dachau and witnessed the atrocities committed there. The scene was shocking and inhumane, even to battle-hardened soldiers, and Patton's troops assumed a new ruthlessness in chasing and fighting the enemy. They were anxious to keep the Germans on the run.

The prisoners, while in camp, had managed to contact the Allies with their manufactured two-way radio, and give their position and the strength of the guards. They worked out a password, and if an attempt was made to eliminate the prisoners, a building was to be set on fire, and fighter planes would give immediate cover, day and night. The German guards, sensing the impending capitulation, used the prison camp for protection to keep from being bombed and strafed.

It was later learned that the German High Command's intent was to eliminate all prisoners.

The General ordered the troops to remain in camp while mop-up operations were continuing. Until transportation arrangements could be made, the men stayed in camp. C rations and K rations were distributed, and the men enjoyed an almost decent meal for the first time in months. The prisoners did break into the adjoining kitchen looking for food, but there was a meager supply. The prisoners found they could eat only small amounts of the rations, since their stomachs had been conditioned to two years of very small quantities of watery soup.

The result of their forced diet was evident. When Hartley Westbrook entered the service he weighed 165 pounds. One week after his release from Stalag VII he weighed 118 pounds.

CHAPTER SEVENTEEN
HOME AT LAST

In early May 1944, the airmen were taken to a nearby Luftwaffe fighter base at Landshut Bavaria, loaded into C-46s and taken to a processing camp in Belgium. Here they were deloused, given hot showers, haircuts, sharp razors, a warm meal and a warm bed. The staff at the camp were very respectful, considerate and caring. After their ordeal the POWs felt they were being "treated like kings," something they had not felt for two years. They were processed and paid some of their wages. A trip to the Post Exchange found new uniforms, underwear, new socks, and new shoes. Their clothing looked new, smelled new, felt new and they felt really clean for the first time. Clean not only in body, but also in spirit.

Some distance from the camp, several columns of smoke appeared on the horizon. The prisoners' clothing, that had been cared for, repaired, occasionally washed, and their only protection from the elements for two years, was being burned.

A few days later the released prisoners flew to Camp Lucky Strike in Le Harve, France, to make arrangements to return to the United States. There were over twenty thousand tents set up, and the airmen were instructed "to find an empty tent and a chow line." Consuming food was still a problem, and the main diet was drinking eggnog, lots of eggnog, since they could not digest regular food yet. It was thirty days before Hap could keep a meal down. It was almost a year before Hap could eat a full meal without difficulty.

Several days later they boarded a victory ship, loaded with released prisoners and food. They joined a one hundred ship convoy, left Port Le Harve, and traveled well out of the submarine lanes. Although it was late in the war the submarine menace continued, and it would have been a cruel fate to have these men who had endured so much be torpedoed on the way home.

Five days later the convoy landed in Boston Harbor. A ticker tape parade was arranged, and the ex-prisoners were treated to a grand welcome with a riding parade down the streets of Boston. From there they were flown to Terre Haute, Indiana, for final processing before leave.

STANDARD TIME INDICATED		THIS IS A FULL RATE TELEGRAM, CABLE-
RECEIVED AT		GRAM OR RADIOGRAM UNLESS OTHERWISE
MAIN OFFICE		INDICATED BY SYMBOL IN THE PREAMBLE
608 LOCUST STREET		OR IN THE ADDRESS OF THE MESSAGE.
PHONE 3-5131		SYMBOLS DESIGNATING SERVICE SELECTED
		ARE OUTLINED IN THE COMPANY'S TARIFFS
TELEPHONE YOUR TELEGRAMS		ON HAND AT EACH OFFICE AND ON FILE WITH
TO POSTAL TELEGRAPH		REGULATORY AUTHORITIES.

Form 14

DS**CB65   C**CDA4 C3 C**NF17 RAD NYJ141N EFM WIRELESS VIA MRT
=N AMFYAS NFD   MAY 17 AM 9 !9
MRS JANE WESTBROOK=
(COONRAPIDS IOWA)

ALL WELL AND SAFE FONDEST LOVE AND KISSED WRITING=
    HARTLEY A WESTBROOK

Postal telegraph sent by Hap upon release from prison, and completing processing. The POW camp was secured April 29th, 1944, and the telegram was sent May 17th, 1944.

From Terre Haute, Hap called Jane, who immediately took a train to meet him in Dayton, OH. In Dayton they boarded a C-47 and flew to Chicago, where they boarded a train to Muscatine, Iowa, and were met by Benjamin and Mabel Westbrook.

How do you greet someone with whom you honeymooned for ten days, and who was then absent for over two years? What do you first say to someone you have not shared a word with for two years? How tightly do you hold someone you love that you feared you would never see again? Is what is unsaid more important than what is said? Can that time ever be made up?

Jane and Hap spent several days in Letts, responding to those questions. There were thousands of young airmen, eighteen, nineteen, twenty years old, buried in Europe who would never have the opportunity to respond to those questions.

When Jane and Hap returned to the Bowers' farm to visit, Jane's uncle, Dr. Irwin, a dentist in Richland, Iowa, organized a "welcome home-victory" dinner in Hap's honor. There was a large turnout for the "war hero," a true celebration with adulation in great abundance. A sumptuous dinner was served and excitement filled

WESTERN UNION

Received at

MR 23 Govt Washington DC 242AM 30

Mrs Jane A Westbrook
Coon Rapids Iowa

The secretary of war desires me to inform you that your husband
1 Lt Westbrook Hartley A returned to military control 29
april 45.

J A Ulio the Adj Genl of the Army

Notification of taking control of the POW camp and acknowledging Hap was once again in the active military and no longer a German prisoner.

the room. After about five bites of the conventional but "rich" food, Hap's stomach reacted violently, and he vomited on his plate. It was extremely embarrassing for Hap, but he had no control over a stomach so deprived for so long.

They spent sixty days visiting friends and family before returning to service. Hap received orders to report to Miami, Florida, where they spent another thirty days in "medical recuperation" in an elegant hotel. Relaxing in the warm sun, walking along the beach, Hap slowly regained his strength, his health, and he and Jane discussed the options for their future life together.

It also afforded Jane and Hap thirty days of honeymoon they were previously denied.

.

CHAPTER EIGHTEEN
IN THE "AIRPORT BUSINESS"

This photo of Hap taken after the war, with his Captain's bars and medals.

With a military obligation to fulfill, orders were received, and Hap reported for duty to decommission Hondo Air Force Base in Texas, where he was reintroduced to training and flying. The duty included relocating airplanes and closing down the facility. Since military responsibilities consumed most of his time, Jane decided to return to Iowa. She continued her opportunity to teach in the Bayard School system and taught second grade while Hap completed his military commitment. Hap managed to return periodically to dispel the loneliness of a pregnant schoolteacher.

Hap was then assigned to decommission the base at Liberal, Kansas, where their main duty was to ferry new bombers to Walnut Ridge Air Force Base in Arkansas. The pilots would then return to Liberal in a C-47 for another trip. Their second trip back Hap was the pilot, and about a half-hour after takeoff encountered a violent snowstorm. It called for emergency measures, and they managed to find an alternate field at Little Rock, where they landed in zero visibility and sat out the storm. Upon returning to Liberal, Kansas, Hap was carrying a parachute that had not been checked out. The prospect of being caught bringing a parachute on base would have created a problem, so Hap wrapped it and sent it home to avoid the hassle.

Several trips were made delivering new B-24s to Kingman, Arizona. At Kingman the new airplanes were dismantled and cut up for scrap. It was very ironic. The 44th Bomber Group was the first contingent of B-24 bombers sent to England, and there was a lamentable lack of bombers to fill out the squadrons. Now, his first assignment was to deliver new bombers for their destruction, planes that had never experienced combat or even a long flight. Originally there were over 18,000 B-24s built to meet the demands of the war. Today, in 2001, there are twelve B-24 airplanes on exhibit, and only three B-24s are operational, and they are privately owned.

In addition to his other duties, through the Lend Lease Program Hap was given the responsibility to teach Chinese pilots how to fly bombers. Captain Westbrook was also assigned to transport, ferrying Very Important Persons around the country in C-47s. The routine of "safe" flying made Hap feel he was not contributing to the war effort.

Since the Air Force was still conducting air raids over Japan, Hap volunteered to become a B-29 pilot in the Pacific Theater. Hap had a strong commitment to serve and complete the war, a war in which he had not had the opportunity to complete his first tour of thirty-five missions. He was not accepted to fly B-29s because the Air Force felt a pilot did not warrant double jeopardy, i.e. the possibility of exposing personnel to becoming a prisoner of war twice.

One of Westbrook's transport flights was flying a C-47 with a cargo destined for Hamilton Air Force Base in California. The plane was stacked solidly with packing crates, and they were also carrying eighteen passengers. They flew to Denver where they spent the night, and the plane was placed under armed guard. The next morning they flew to Salt Lake City, Utah, refueled and then headed west to Sacramento. About mid-flight Hap turned the controls over to the co-pilot, and crawled on the cargo boxes to catch forty winks. Suddenly the plane started acting up, and Hap ran forward to the cockpit and took over as pilot, since he was charged with the flight. The plane had high carburetor heat and low manifold pressure. They had lost pressurization in the cabin and it was necessary to lose altitude. Over Lake Tahoe, they dropped to 150 feet, assessed the situation and made the necessary adjustments.

However, they still had to fly over Donner Pass at 13,000 feet.

He radioed Sacramento about their predicament, and the Commanding General demanded to know their position and how far they were from Hamilton Base.

When Hap was about three miles out he contacted the base, and they were directed to land and taxi to a remote corner of the field. An armed escort directed them to a specified location and when finally stopped, they were told to open the cargo doors and not exit any of the passengers off the plane. The plane was greeted by a General who proceeded to check all the forms and then directed the unloading of the boxes. It seems they had been hauling valuable parts for nuclear warheads, and the General was quite concerned over their whereabouts.

Westbrook continued escorting VIPs around the country until April 1947, when he was discharged from service.

What does a flying officer do when he no longer has stable employment? How does one "settle in" and start generating income to support a wife and family?

More importantly, HOW DO YOU GENERATE INCOME IN THE AIRPORT BUSINESS?

Westbrook was contacted by American Airlines, which in 1947 was just getting started in the passenger business in a big way. The airlines were in need of experienced four engine aircraft pilots, and Hap had lots of air hours on his resume. He chose, instead, to become an air-

Captain Westbrook and friend in front of a C-46 Transport after being recalled into service during the Korean Conflict. Flying VIPs was too boring, as Hap wanted to return to run the Atlantic Airport.

port operator and offer flying lessons. It was his opportunity to teach and to "coach." He continued as a member of the Air Force Reserve, and once a month had the opportunity to keep current on the changing nature of military aircraft.

He was looking for a job, and found one in Guthrie Center, Iowa, a rural county seat town of 1,600 people just a stone's throw from Bayard. With a grass runway and no facilities, it proved to be a real challenge. Housing was reasonably priced, there was an interest in flying, and Hap struggled to start a charter service.

Westbrook had the backing of the community leaders who recognized the desirability of the town having a functioning airport. The following article appeared under a two-column picture of Westbrook on the front page of the Guthrie Center Times, (A Farmers Newspaper) in 1948. It stated:

"H. A. Westbrook "Hap," manager of the municipal airport, is pictured above shortly before he took off with the mail for the Guthrie Center Times. For the past month Westbrook has been delivering the Times by special airmail to the towns of Bagley, Bayard and Coon Rapids every Thursday afternoon. The service was inaugurated by the Times because of the inability of postal service to get the papers to those towns for delivery by Friday despite the fact that none of them are more than 20 miles distant. Postal authorities were unable to offer solution other than truck or air delivery and permission for Westbrook to carry the Times by air was granted. When you see one of the local planes heading north Thursday afternoons around 4:30 o'clock that's Westbrook carrying the mail."

The same paper carried three additional newsy items under [News of Municipal Airport].

"Believe it or not, one of the planes based at the local airport took off without a pilot Saturday night, then came to a landing atop the office building. Explanation for this freakish stunt lay in the strong wind of that night which picked up the plane, tie-down stakes and all, and parked it on the roof of the building. The plane, one of three belonging to the city, suffered approximately one hundred dollars damage."

MA

"Earl Springer joined the exclusive group of Guthrie Center birdmen last week by taking up a Cub on his first flight."

MA

"Now that H. A. Westbrook, airport manager, has purchased a new plane for the airport, anyone interested in buying a J3-F60 Cub for a reasonable price can find one at the airport."

Westbrook's enthusiasm and salesmanship were front page material in Guthrie Center. In 1949, Westbrook arranged with Cessna of Wichita, Kansas, to market their aircraft. Cessna was one of the better managed airplane manufacturing companies, and Cessna and Hap developed a long-lasting working relationship.

After two years in Guthrie Center, the city fathers of Atlantic, Iowa, another county seat community of 7,000 persons, contacted Westbrook to manage their airport. Atlantic was an active, growing community in Southwest Iowa, and had potential for a thriving airport. After discussing the proposition with Jane, they accepted the offer and proceeded to move. While making arrangements to move in 1950 the Korean conflict broke out, and Captain Westbrook was recalled to active duty in the Air Force. Hap was forced to leave his young family, and was assigned to Offut Air Base in Omaha Nebraska, about sixty miles from Atlantic.

Westbrook's assignment was, once again, to fly VIPs around the country in C-46s and C-47s. There was a need for B-50 and B-52 pilots, so Hap again volunteered and was sent to March Field, California, for training. It meant an overseas assignment, and after some thought and considering separation from the family, Hap left the bomber command and was assigned to refueling operations. Large cargo planes filled with aviation gasoline would meet bombers at midpoint of their mission and re-fuel in mid-flight to extend their range. It was demanding and exacting flying.

Hap was placed on reserve with assignments becoming less numerous, and the boredom of waiting was debilitating to the young airman, so he decided to resign his commission. He contacted his Senator, Bourke Hickenlooper (Rep, IA), and with the Senator's help managed to obtain a discharge so he could return to Atlantic to start the new enterprise.

Westbrook was contacted a short time later by Colonel Milford Juhl of Boone, Iowa, who had been appointed by the Governor of Iowa and given the task of forming the Iowa National Air Guard. Juhl offered Westbrook the opportunity to be the first pilot in the INAG and Chief Pilot. With the opportunity to serve long enough to gain a retirement pension, Hap decided to join the Guard as its first operational pilot and help organize the State operation.

As Chief Pilot in the Iowa National Air Guard he became the second helicopter pilot in the state. Practically every weekend he participated in flight breakfasts around the state, giving demonstrations on helicopter performance and generally promoting the Air Guard. He then spent hours teaching recruits how to fly military helicopters of all types. Westbrook additionally was Battalion Commander of installations at Boone, Waterloo and Davenport. Hap retired from the Air Guard in 1968 with the rank of Lieutenant Colonel.

Participating in flight breakfasts around the state gave Westbrook the opportunity to show his prowess flying a helicopter, which was a relatively new aircraft at that time. He amazed the crowds by tipping over a fifty-five gallon drum, rolling it around with the aircraft skids, then tipping it back upright. He would then put a skid on the top of the drum and pivot the rotorcraft, without tipping over the drum.

Westbrook Delivers Times by Air

Hap once started a lecture to a group of pilot trainees with, "You don't know what flying is until you've lost the rotor propeller on a Hiller H-23 helicopter."

Hartley Westbrook shown with his airplane on the front page of the Guthrie Center newspaper on April 10th, 1947. (photo: Guthrie Center Times)

CHAPTER NINETEEN
HOME IN ATLANTIC

Reverting to an earlier question, HOW DO YOU MAKE MONEY OPERATING AN AIRPORT?

Hap and Jane learned early. You do whatever it takes.

The move to Atlantic was not easy for Jane. Suddenly her world was much more complicated. They lived in a small white house at the airport, and since Hap was scrambling to build a charter service, give lessons, participate in the Iowa Air Guard, and attend weekend fly-ins, a great deal of responsibility for airport operation fell on Jane's shoulders.

They had started their family when Hap had returned from Europe. Son John Hartley was born March 3, 1946, at St Anthony's Hospital in Carroll, Iowa. Daughter Diana Jane (named after Hap's airplane but misspelled) was born in Guthrie Center on November 18, 1949. Daughter Judy Lynn was born on March 2, 1952, while Hap was serving during the Korean conflict.

Richard Edward was born in Atlantic July 22, 1954. And Jeanie Luann was born in Atlantic, October 24, 1957.

Jane was not only raising the family, but was a frontier woman coping with the relatively new concept of small town fixed-base

With new son John, Jane and Hap prepare for Hap's recall into service during the Korean Conflict.

operation. Hap was giving lessons, and flying occasional charter service. This meant that Jane was in charge of operating the facility in Hap's absence, which occurred frequently. While Hap was away almost every weekend promoting flying and the Iowa National Air Guard at fly-ins, Jane raised the children, serviced transient aircraft, pumped gas, filed reports, bought insurance, wrote checks and kept the books.

Living in a small house located on airport property meant dealing with problems twenty-four hours a day. Buying a new home in a nice neighborhood gave Jane some relief, but her job description did not change.

The first task for a successful airport operation was to create the need of the community for airport utilization. The Atlantic City Council was not quite as enthusiastic about their airport as Guthrie Center had been. The support for an all-weather surface runway and a new hangar was extracted from the Council, but not without considerable effort.

As the years passed, Hap was enthusiastically supported by the community, and he and Jane actively participated in community activities.

When Hap asked the Council for additional funds, the Council permitted him to farm the land around the airport runway and apply the income to Hap's needs. Hap bought a Fordson tractor to till the ground, and pushed snow off the runway with a blade mounted on his pickup truck. He slowly acquired the necessary equipment to meet the needs for towing airplanes, the tools to repair airplanes, and the reputation to service all aspects of aircraft.

Hap signed on with Cessna to sell their aircraft. Certain manufacturers like Beechcraft and Taylorcraft established sales territories, which were rigidly honored by salesmen. Cessna did not establish territories, which meant Westbrook could sell airplanes nationwide. On charter flights and numerous trips, Hap managed to establish relationships of trust which enabled him to sell, trade and conduct business over a larger area. Westbrook sold planes manufactured by Beechcraft, Taylorcraft, Cessna, Mooney, Avion, Aircoupe, Piper, and a few planes of questionable parentage.

A local barber was an avid hunter and talked to Hap about the prospect of hunting coyotes from the air. Coyotes were quite abundant in western Iowa, a real nuisance, and there was a bounty of twenty-five dollars per head. Hap equipped his plane with skis, and during one winter he and his barber friend harvested more than two hundred twenty five coyotes, splitting the bounty. This lasted several years, until a law was passed banning hunting from aircraft.

A pilot from the adjoining town of Clarinda thought this was a good idea and tried it with a local hunter. They proceeded to shoot off their airplane's propeller because of inept plane handling and an over-eager response upon spotting a coyote.

Jane continued to raise the family and became interested in the local Parent Teacher Association. She soon was president of the Atlantic Chapter, and looking for more involvement, became active in the State Chapter. She ultimately served as State President of the PTA, and remained active for several years, serving on the State Board.

Jane was also active in Eastern Star, serving as Worthy Matron for the local organization. She was also active in the Daughters of the American Revolution. All this while raising five children, pumping gas, and running the "airport store." Jane and Hap additionally found time to belong to several bridge clubs in town, where they proved to be formidable competitors.

During this same period Hap became active in the Masonic Order.

Hap needed money to buy an airplane. Bankers, however, had no experience in the fledgling aircraft business, and were less than enthusiastic about considering any loan on a flying machine. Loaning money on tractors and plows they understood, but bankers had a difficult time grasping aircraft finance under the then current banking practices. Since the City Council permitted Westbrook to farm the land surrounding the airport, he decided to go into the cattle business. He arranged for a farm loan to buy eighty head of cattle. Hap proceeded to western Nebraska where he bought eighty head of cattle, then took out a second mortgage using the cattle as collateral to get the money to buy an airplane.

With characteristic farm savvy he proceeded to sell the airplane, take another plane in trade, and sold it, making a fair profit on both sales. The cattle, however, did not respond to his "farm savvy." They contracted pink eye, requiring large veterinarian bills, and as a result, were sold at a loss.

When Hap again approached the banker explaining what had happened, the banker replied, "Stay out of the cattle business. I have money for airplanes any time you need it." Hap went on to be one of Cessna's best customers and has the longest continuing dealership in Cessna's history.

The Westbrooks continued to develop their reputation as fair and capable operators. One day a plane flown by a businessman on his way to Des Moines made an emergency landing in Atlantic. Jane parked the plane, and offered the businessman her car so he could continue on to attend his business meeting. When Hap returned from his charter he repaired the plane, and when the businessman returned from Des Moines he was pleased to discover he could return home without waiting. Paying a modest amount for the plane repair, he continued on his way singing the praises of the Atlantic operation.

Jane Westbrook was a very generous person in her own way. She believed that you "give and you get." She was interested in the friends of her children, perhaps a bit too much. Whenever the girls would break up with a boyfriend, she insisted on inviting the past boyfriends to all the family parties and also the girls' weddings, much to the dismay of the young ladies.

One time a young man passing through Atlantic was seriously burned in an automobile accident. Although they had never met, Jane visited him every day during his stay in the hospital until he was released.

The dining room table was the meeting place for the family, and there were usually one or two extra plates at the table for those who happened to drop by, whether they were pilots, school chums, old boy friends, or casual acquaintances. Jane had an unusual sense of humor, which appeared at various times in interesting ways. She was always eating off other people's plates (just a taste!), which frankly, "drove the children up the wall." (Never eat a sandwich in front of Jane!) She was known to give Christmas presents in October (it was a good buy!). She was known to put plastic wrap across the toilet bowl just to see if people were paying attention.

Her children observed that it was impossible for her to back out of the garage without hitting something. At a family gathering at Diana's house there were several cars parked in the driveway. Diana's husband, Robert, had just purchased a new pick-up truck with fancy Corvette racing hubcaps. As Jane was leaving the gathering backing her car down the driveway, she clipped off both hubcaps on the drivers side without touching the body of the pick-up truck. Close inspection indicated it was impossible to hit a hubcap without scraping the side of the pick-up, but Jane managed to pull it off.

Jane loved to drive fast. On one trip Jane was driving to Denver with Diana, and upon reaching Omaha, stopped at a red light at 13th Street, just across the Iowa bridge. Two young men pulled alongside in a "muscle car," racing their engine. Jane responded to the challenge, and when the light turned green they proceeded to drag race at full speed for the next fourteen miles to Exit 443 on the west side of Omaha. There the young men decided Lincoln was too far away to race, turned around, and headed back to town.

In the late 1950s the rural roads were not the fully developed farm-to-market roads as they are today. Cass County soil was yellow clay, topped by a thin layer of black loam. The roadbeds were clay with little or no gravel. When dry, the roadbed was as hard and solid as concrete. When wet, the roadbeds were slippery, soft and nearly impassable. During the winter, a heavy snow would isolate farmsteads for weeks at a time.

After one snowstorm, a local resident in charge of delivering the *Sunday Des Moines Register* on rural routes called Hap and asked if it would be possible to deliver the paper by air. Hap assured him it was very possible and flew the route, chucking the paper out of the low flying airplane. The experiment was so successful he continued to deliver the large Sunday paper by airdrop.

On one occasion he flew low over a farmstead and accidentally dropped the paper down the brick chimney. When the farmer got up in the morning and started the fire in the kitchen stove, it refused to draw. Removing the metal flue, he discovered his Sunday paper. He immediately called Hap and thanked him for not

Delivering the Sunday paper by air was a unique occurrence. Farmers who were isolated by muddy roads or snow drifts appreciated the uncanny accuracy of Hap's delivery.

only delivering the paper, but also for cleaning his brick chimney flue.

On another occasion a farmer kidded that it would help if Hap could put the paper on the porch so the farmer would not have to get dressed for winter to retrieve the paper from a snowdrift. The next delivery, Hap proceeded to fly low and tossed it toward the side porch. The paper bounced off the icy porch floor, crashed through a window and landed at the feet of the farmer who was sitting at the kitchen table drinking coffee. This, of course, made

Hap's reputation, and the farmer told the story with great glee. The farmer's wife, however, was upset because they had to replace the window, and she let Hap know about it publicly. In today's world it would probably generate a lawsuit.

A member of the Federal Aeronautics Association (FAA), which was becoming more influential in the aircraft industry, contacted Hap about his newspaper delivery. At the time unidentified flying objects (UFOs) were dominating the news, and the FAA was investigating all sorts of aeronautical aberrations. The investigator asked Hap about the newspaper delivery and asked to see a demonstration.

Hap wrapped several newspapers with a rubber band, and they took off searching for a target. When they spotted a tractor pulling a disc, the inspector said, "Let's try that tractor for a target." Hap, looking down at the sixteen-foot wide disc, replied, "Do you want the disc or the tractor?" The inspector allowed that a fifty-foot radius would be adequate. Hap was firm, "No, either the tractor or the disc." The Inspector said, "OK. Try the disc."

Hap slowed the plane down to ninety miles per hour and at five hundred feet launched the paper. It bounced off the disc, forward, and was chewed up as the disc rolled over it. Hap said, "Do you want to see another one?"

The inspector replied, "That's good enough for me. Let's get back."

An Iowa Pilot Named Hap

CHAPTER TWENTY
GROWING, LEARNING & TEACHING

Hap's Air Service was hired to fly members of the National Farmers Organization to various meetings around the country. The NFO and its leader, Orren Lee Staley, were quite controversial, due to their attempts to organize a farmer's union for marketing farm products. The NFO became one of Hap's steadiest customers. As they traveled the country they were met with opposition in several forms. At one stop after a meeting they left the airfield, and the airplane started acting up requiring an emergency landing at Beloit, Kansas. They learned that someone had poured sugar in the gas tanks. Thereafter, any stop required security for the airplane.

The NFO ultimately purchased two airplanes from Hap for its use. One, unfortunately, crashed on takeoff after only twenty-two hours of flying time.

Brown Shoe-Fit also became a regular client as their charter business expanded.

In his own way Hap was sort of a control freak. When he assigned a task it was to be done. There was no more conversation. When the Atlantic Airport was under-funded, he did not complain. He rolled up his sleeves, raised corn and beans and made ends meet. When the city refused to buy runway snow equipment, Hap purchased a blade for his pickup and moved the snow. When he wanted a hangar he read up on steel buildings, bought the parts, and erected it himself.

Hap had simple rules. Go to work at 8:00 a.m., not 8:01 a.m. No emotion, just get the work done. Things don't get done if you don't go out and do it. He continued the can-do attitude which had earned him respect in the military.

One day Hap loaded young Dick, age five, in the airplane and went flying. They finally landed in Oklahoma City at the Wiley Post Airfield. Hap was in Oklahoma to inspect a wrecked Cessna 320 twin-engine aircraft, owned by a doctor from California. The wings had been cut off one foot from the fuselage, severing all the electrical wires one foot from a junction box. The plane was repairable, but not without considerable effort. After some negotiation, Hap and Dick returned to Atlantic. Hap admonished his son, "Don't tell Mom what we've done."

About a week later, the family was sitting down for dinner when they received a phone call from a local restaurant. A waitress was on the line and said, "You'd better hurry down here. There is a fellow with an airplane on a truck at the gas station looking for you." So much for a well kept secret.

The repair of the airplane took over a year and one-half. All of the electrical wires were white (before color-coding was used) and reconstructing the plane was very laborious. Dick remembers being cramped and sore from riveting the plane, since he was the only one small enough to get into the tight corners. The salesman later said that there were only one or two persons in the U.S. who could rebuild a plane in that condition. When it was completed, it passed FAA inspections with flying colors. The plane's first use was flying an accident victim with serious injuries from Atlantic to a Des Moines hospital on Christmas Eve. Hap used the plane in his operations for many years, until it literally fell apart.

During this period Hap felt it necessary to continue to grow professionally. In 1958, as busy as he was, he completed a correspondence course and received an A & P Mechanic Certificate with Aircraft Inspector Authorization. He later became a FAR 135 Air Taxi Check Airman. He was already a FAA Designated Examiner.

How do you make a living at a small town airport? Hap and Jane looked at their surroundings and extracted as much as they could. In 1965 they had a call from a client in Honduras who wanted a new airplane. Hap ordered the new plane, and he and Jane picked it up at the factory and delivered it. Their maps went only to the Texas border. They did have a map of Brownsville, Texas, and on the other side was a map of the western hemisphere. They followed the coastline to Honduras, found the city of Tegucigalpa, located the airport and landed at night in a driving rainstorm.

The commercial flight back on a DC-6 made Hap most uncomfortable since the pilot could not properly synchronize the engines. Hap resisted a mid-air flying lesson since he suspected the engines were too worn to be properly coordinated.

In 1966, Westbrook was contacted by Iowa Western Community College in Council Bluffs, Iowa, and asked to develop a course in Aircraft Maintenance. Hap discovered that there was not a textbook available, so he prepared an outline for teaching Basic Aviation Mechanics, Basic Electric and Electrical Systems, Fuel and Fuel Systems, and FAA Requirements for Air Frame and Power Plant Technicians. He assembled an advisory committee to guide the course, as well as all the tools, engines, and teaching devices necessary for an accredited program. He continued to teach at the Community College until 1974, when he relocated to Ames.

In 1974 Hap and Jane received a 25-year-award for representing and selling Cessna aircraft. Hap had successfully marketed the aviation industry, and Cessna rewarded him with a mounting of 25 silver dollars, one for every year he represented the company.

Hap and Jane were in Atlantic for twenty-four years promoting flying, giving lessons, chartering, reducing the coyote population, delivering newspapers, serving as a volunteer fireman and election officers, organizing Cub Scout packs, and contributing to the community through a number of other activities. They owned five airplanes and had sold and serviced many, many more.

In 1974 at a special recognition dinner, Cessna President Duane Wallace presented Jane and Hap Westbrook with twenty-five silver dollars mounted on a plaque for their twenty-five years of selling and servicing Cessna aircraft.

CHAPTER TWENTY-ONE
AMES

In 1975, Hap and Jane had the opportunity to move their operation to the Ames Airport. Ames was the home of Iowa State University and several large companies. The community of forty-five thousand had many more options available for this hardworking pair. A more affluent community with several flying clubs and a glider club, their opportunity was enhanced by a number of the twenty-two thousand students at ISU interested in learning to fly.

The previous operator had left problems to deal with. He had built a hangar with limited resources and was ready to default on the loan. The operator had sold a number of Cessna aircraft with lessons included in the sale and could not meet those obligations. Hap made arrangements to assume all of these obligations, which meant commitment without cash flow. It was a rocky time, but the effort built a great deal of goodwill and trust.

To improve his capabilities and serve the community better, he spent over 140 hours in correspondence school on Airport Operations. That course along with his Aircraft Maintenance Certification and Official Aircraft Inspector authorization enhanced his capability for flight instruction, charter services, and maintenance services to the central Iowa area.

The May 1st move to Ames created one minor family problem. Daughter Jeanie was spending her senior year in high school abroad in South Africa. Jeanie was special, because as a child she was born with a leg deformity that required corrective surgery and several operations. The end result, after several trying years, was most successful. Being the youngest child, she was always especially loved by the family.

Planning to move in early spring, Jane decided she did not want Jeanie to return from South Africa to a new community, but to the home she remembered. Jane chose to remain in Atlantic until Jeanie's return, then sold the house and joined Hap in Ames.

The entire family was involved in the operations in one way or another. While in Atlantic, son Dick attended Northwest Missouri State College and graduated in 1976. In 1975 at the end of the school year, Dick received a call from Hap one midnight and was informed that he was to report to Ames to run the airport the next morning. Hap had just bought a new house, and Dick was to drive to Ames, find the house and sleep in the basement on a mattress. Without knowing the community, Dick drove around Ames for several hours in the middle of the night before finding the house, the basement and the mattress.

When Dick arrived at the Ames airport, there were two airplanes on the line. In later years all lines would be full, and Hap's Air Service would own as many as 22 aircraft to meet his business needs.

Dick's association with his father, both while growing up and in business, was always "strictly business." Dick never once heard a "war story" from his father, who was always guarded about his military and POW experience. Hap did not like to dwell on the past, but was concerned with getting the job done.

One day at the airport Dick was making pilot conversation with a friend, discussing how high they had flown. During the discussion Dick indicated he had flown a private jet at 45,000 feet, and the conversation continued for a half-hour longer. Hap suddenly interjected, "I was assigned to see how high a B-24 would fly as a tactical appraisal of German fighter planes. I stalled it out at 39,500 feet." This was Dick's first and last "war story," until a newspaper article appeared in the Ames Tribune about Hap's Operator of The Year Award in 1989.

As operations increased at the Ames airport, improvements were made. In 1979-80 a localizer approach (LOC) and distance measuring equipment (DME) were added to runway 31. The city also purchased new snow removal equipment and built additional airplane storage hangers.

A year later, a taxiway was added to runway 310. In 1984, the grass runway 01/19 was paved. It was later extended to 5700 feet to accommodate small jets that were increasingly active in the area. Additional taxiways and tie-downs were also added.

Jane was a sports nut. She loved football, and many Sunday dinners were scheduled around the halftime or starting times of her favorite teams. When Johnny Orr became head basketball coach at

ISU, she energetically embraced a new sport. The team regularly flew from the airport, and Jane developed a motherly attitude toward the team. She often gave Coach Orr advice on how to play Kansas and Missouri, and was convinced she was an expert on basketball. When the team lost a close game she would send flowers to Coach Orr with an encouraging message. She participated in a bridge club with Coach Orr's wife Romie, and felt this gave her license to give the coach advice.

The activity generated by a Big Eight/Big Twelve community meant a more active charter service. With political figures regularly zipping in and out of town, charter service was thriving. The list of VIPs flown by Hap's Air Service is long and impressive. They would include, but are not limited to: members of the Kennedy family, Bob Dole, Elizabeth Dole, Senators Charles Grassley and Tom Harkin, most of the Iowa congressional delegation, and most candidates for presidential elections attending the Iowa caucuses. He flew governors, business leaders, architects, engineers, chamber executives, and coaches on recruiting trips.

After one basketball game, the Kansas basketball team and Coach Larry Brown were delayed in their takeoff from the Ames airport because of snow on the runway. While waiting for the snow plows to complete their task, Coach Brown discovered he did not have enough cash to take the team to dinner. Jane Westbrook loaned Coach Brown money so they could visit a local fast food restaurant for burgers and cokes for the team. Whether Jane offered coaching advice to Coach Brown is not known. It might have helped, since Coach Larry Brown never won a game in Ames during his tenure as basketball coach at Kansas University.

As the children grew they were encouraged to learn to play a musical instrument. Son John played the cornet and trumpet and participated in the marching band. Jeanie and Judy played the piano and the drums, Diana played clarinet, and Dick played the drums. While living in Atlantic with the children participating in music lessons, Hap purchased and tried to learn to play the accordion. His inconsistent efforts culminated in learning to play "Three Blind Mice." The instrument is still in Hap's possession, and the family fears for an accordion revival and an attempt to play "Lady of Spain."

As the airport operation continued, Hap's Air Service continued to build goodwill. If a pilot was passing through Ames after regular hours and needed service, they would leave the gas cap unlocked and tell the pilot to help himself. In twenty years of operation Hap was never taken advantage of by transient pilots.

The airport would frequently receive calls from airline pilots passing overhead to "say hello to the man who taught me how to fly." Pilots flying over Ames would land to have a cup of coffee with "my old instructor." The fraternity of pilots is close and associations long-lasting.

Ames Airport became the busiest uncontrolled airport in the state, and was the third busiest airport in the state. This effort was rewarded in 1989 when Hartley Westbrook was selected the Airport Operator of the Year by the Flying Farmers of America.

Jane and son John were very close. John was a natural born salesman. Early on he had joined the family operation, and represented Hap's Air Service in several locations. John married Marla Berman, from Cincinnati, Ohio, in 1973. John built a successful aircraft sales business in Greeley, CO, and Des Moines, and ultimately moved to Denver with Marla and their three children Daniel, Jamie Michelle, and Carey Rebecca. Since Marla was of the Jewish faith, John obligingly converted to Judaism. John loved the outdoors, hunting and fishing, and particularly flying. He was an excellent pilot and flying was an extension of the freedom of the great outdoors.

John called his mother every day. Jane was perceived by the family not only as a mother, but also as a best friend, and not only by the family, but by most of the people in the community. John's phone calls were not extended, but a way to keep in touch, and current.

Early in the morning, on May 2nd, 1991, John took off from a Denver airport at 6:48 am in his Piper Navajo twin-engine aircraft on a sales trip. He called his mother and made a date for lunch, since his flight plan was close to Ames. At 6:51 a.m., he called the airport tower to report that a cowling had come loose on one of the engines. They later learned that the cowling had been closed by a mechanic, but not latched. At 6:53 a.m., John attempted an emergency landing eleven miles from the airport, crashing the airplane into the ground and killing him instantly.

Hap and Jane never fully recovered from the loss of their son. Life went on. Business went on. The rest of the family grew and prospered. But there would always be that unstated void in Jane and Hap's life from John's accidental death.

As P.O.W.s grew older there was new interest in rekindling friendships and sharing stories. Organizations were formed, and newsletters were printed with letters and accounts of service incidents.

CHAPTER TWENTY-TWO
REUNIONS

In 1984, Jane, Jeanie, and Hap returned to England to an Eighth Air Force Reunion, and visited Shipdham and the surrounding area. Many of the airfields in "Little America" have been removed. However, the main runways remain at Shipdham, as does the dilapidated two-story control tower. Funds are now being raised to restore the control tower as an Eighth Air Force Museum, recording the activity from 1941 to 1945.

Working around airplanes all of his life had taken its toll on Hap's physical condition. Because of under-funding at Atlantic and Ames, equipment for lifting heavy objects was not available, and it was all done by hand. As a result, the cartilage loss in Hap's shoulders required shoulder bone replacement. In 1988, Hap went to the Mayo Clinic in Rochester and had a shoulder replaced. Jane accompanied him and would not let anyone visit him.

In 1993, the second shoulder had to be replaced, and Hap visited his doctor who had moved to Minneapolis. This time he wanted no assistance from the family and traveled to Minneapolis with a friend from Ames who used the same doctor. After two days in the hospital after the operation, Hap could not wait to get out and called his daughter Diana and granddaughter Christa to come pick him up. Hap could not waste time recuperating and had to get back to work.

The doctor told Hap not to drive a car for ten days after surgery, but the first day at home Hap drove his pickup truck to the office. He justified his action saying, "The doctor said car. He didn't mention a truck."

The family continued to participate in Hap's Air Service in Ames. Diana continues to serve as bookkeeper. Diana's husband, Robert Holden, is in aircraft maintenance and is a licensed A & P Mechanic. Dick was airport operations manager from 1975 to 1993, with a brief interlude in Denver. He left in 1993 and now owns an aircraft company dealing in sales, management and pilot services.

Judy and husband Rick Mewhirter live in Dallas, where Judy is a computer technician and Rick is a consultant in hospital management.

Jeanie lives in Ankeny, Iowa, working as a money manager for the Farm Bureau, and her husband Scott Smith sells aircraft insurance.

With Jane and Hap chartering many ISU coaches on their recruiting trips, they gained favored seating at football and basketball games. Their original seats for basketball in Hilton Coliseum were in the balcony, and Hap was offered an opportunity to move to better seats in the parquet seating. Jane refused to move since she did not want to take "other people's property." Dick convinced her they were really her seats, and from the new location her voice could reach the referees. Jane improved her seats and the referees' calls.

Jane smoked all of her life, and in the early 1990s developed emphysema. In 1993, she experienced a light stroke that curtailed her social and active life. Her dependence on oxygen kept her isolated in her home. She was still as feisty as ever, but her energy could not support much physical activity. Hap had always kept his emotions to himself, and concentrated on getting things done. He was well-read and active, but his demeanor was constant. He was as unemotional when he sold his first airplane as he was when he made his most recent sale. He accepted Jane's condition with the same stoicism.

This plaque acknowledging the successes of the 44th Bomb Group, the "Flying Eightballs" was dedicated during Hap's return for the fiftieth reunion of the Bomb Group.

The POW Association planned a fiftieth reunion in Germany in 1995, and since Jane was not able to travel Diana accompanied Hap on the journey. They first flew to Germany and assembled. From there they traveled by bus to Sagan, site of Stalag Luft III. It was a very emotional time for all of the POW's. The buildings were torn down and the fences gone, but the opening in the trees delineated the location of the camp, and ex-prisoners soon could locate the theater site, appel field, ball field and other major features. The ex-prisoners remembered the funny things that had happened and avoided discussing the traumatic times. They visited the local cemetery and saw the graves of the Russian and Polish soldiers eliminated during the American and British march to Moosburg. A small museum displayed artifacts the prisoners had made: the passports, radios, German uniforms, playing cards, and YMCA logbooks.

The only person Hap knew on the trip was a fellow POW from Pella, Iowa, Robert Menning, who was shot down in Tunisia, North Africa. New contacts were made, however, and they continue to share information to this day.

At one POW reunion a German guard from Stalag Luft III attended. The mood of the prisoners was interesting, in that they forgave their captor since he was doing his assigned military job and they understood military assignment. The POWs were much less forgiving to the Germans who denied involvement with the concentration camps.

One of the reporters accompanying the trip made reference to the assembled group of POWs saying "they were heros."

He was corrected by a POW, who stated, "WE WERE NOT HEROS. WE WERE EIGHTEEN, NINETEEN AND TWENTY YEAR OLD KIDS DOING A JOB."

In 1994, the City of Ames employed a consultant to review the status of the airport, since several improvements were being contemplated and funding was uncertain. At that time Westbrook had two contracts with the city. The first contract was as Airport Manager, which made Hap an employee of the City, paying him for mowing the grass, keeping the runways snow-free, keeping the City equipment in good repair, keeping office hours at the Airport and renting hangar storage space. The second contract was as Fixed Base Operator, giving lessons, repairing and maintaining airplanes, and selling airplanes. For this privilege, Westbrook paid rent to the City and had his own employees. These contracts were renewed every five years.

The City acknowledged that much of the success experienced over the years at the Ames Municipal Airport was due to the efforts of Westbrook. However, because of a desire to increase net revenue at the Airport to cover operating and capital costs reflected in the City's new Master Plan, the consultant recommended the decoupling of the two contracts. Under the new scenario, the City took over the responsibility for the Airport Manager functions to reduce expenditures, leaving the FBO activities to be bid out separately. Competitive proposals were solicited, and the Westbrook bid proved not to be the most financially attractive to the City. As a result, the FBO functions were awarded to another operator.

At this time the aircraft industry was experiencing a slow period, and Hap felt the change would penalize him economically. Being aware of the fragile nature of generating income in the "airplane business," Hap took it as a personal affront. This was definitely not the City's intent. The separation was not a happy one and was most disconcerting for Hap after many years of success, building the third busiest airport in the state, after Des Moines and Cedar Rapids.

Hap's Air Service rented and renovated a hanger from Iowa State University on the airport grounds, moved its twenty-two aircraft, and continues to offer instruction, sales and maintenance services to the central Iowa aviation community.

Now in his eighties, Hap goes to the office every day, continues to give flight checks, and flies at every opportunity.

You have a job and you do it.

Hap Westbrook, who at age 81 still goes to the office every day, is surrounded by a lifetime of awards and memorabilia.

On June 7, 2001, Cessna Customer Service Representatives Ronald Chapman and Steve Charles presented Hartley Westbrook with a plaque honoring his fifty-year association with Cessna.

Hap continues to give check rides at every opportunity. Here he inspects an airplane in the process of repair.

CHAPTER TWENTY-THREE
IOWA AVIATION HALL OF FAME

Notification of Hartley Westbrook's pending induction into the Iowa Aviation Hall of Fame was a pleasant surprise. The award recognized persons who had made significant contributions to Iowa Aviation, and in the year 2000 there would be only one recipient of the award.

Hap was nominated for the recognition by his son Dick who forwarded a nomination form to the selection committee. It included a brief biography, list of aviation accomplishments and described incidents relating to airport operations and flying instruction for over forty-five years. The application included the following paragraphs:

"Anyone who has flown across Iowa over the past fifty plus years knows of the legendary service that truly identifies Hap Westbrook. Many are thankful that they could call on him in the middle of the night to clear snow or fuel their airplane. An eastern Iowa construction company still recalls how their plane landed in Atlantic during an ice storm and Hap gave them the family car so they could continue. Many were the flights when he would depart on a charter with blood for the Red Cross, an ambulance patient, or other important persons or cargo, knowing that the weather was forecast to deteriorate so that he couldn't make the return flight home to his family.

"Annually, Christmas cards arrive from all over the globe; customers thanking him for repairing their plane, airline pilots expressing their thanks for Hap giving them their start, and countless cards from new pilots whom have just taken the checkride for their pilot license.

"Hap Westbrook is truly one of 'the grass-roots builders of the General Aviation business...and I thank you for naming him one of 'Iowa's Aviation Pioneers.' He is a true aviator and teacher, and now in his eighties, he never tires of introducing aviation to Iowa. He is my Mentor and my Father."

The 11th annual induction was held Saturday, June 24th, 2000, in Greenfield, Iowa, at the 4-H building on the fairgrounds. The

Greenfield location is apt and appropriate because it has an excellent aviation museum with a number of rare and unique aircraft. There were about one hundred fifty aviation industry enthusiasts in attendance.

The Westbrooks were represented at the induction by seventeen members of the family, including eight grandchildren, three great grandchildren and one nephew.

The program opened with a welcome by Ron Havens, President of the Antique Aircraft Preservation Association, and special recognition was made of a 2000 Friendship Award for individuals contributing to the Museum.

Hartley Westbrook was introduced and spoke for about one-half hour recounting several incidents included in this book. In every speech Hap made he always repeated his favorite quote: *"Our bombers were escorted from our base in England to the English coast by Spitfires, and we were escorted to the target and back by Messerschmitts."*

WESTBROOK'S CREDENTIALS INCLUDE:

* Commercial Pilots Certificate No. 79331 (Issued 1941) Airplane Single and Multi-engine Land

* Commercial Pilots Certificate - Single Engine - Sea

* Commercial Pilots Certificate - Rotorcraft

* Certified Flight Instructor - Airplane, Single and Multi-Engine

* Certified Flight Instructor - Rotorcraft

* Certified Flight Instructor - Instrument

* FAA designated Examiner

* A & P Mechanic Certificate No 1431474 (Issued 1958) with Aircraft Inspector Authorization

* 23 years of Military Service, including two years as a Prisoner of War

* USAF Lt Colonel (Retired)

* Awarded the Purple Heart

* Awarded the Air Medal with two Oak Leaf Clusters
* Awarded the Prisoner of War Medal
* 1989 Airport Operator of the Year by Flying Farmers of Iowa
* Director - Iowa Aviation Business Association
* Cessna Aircraft Dealer for over fifty years - 2nd in most Cessna planes sold world wide
* Operated Guthrie Center Airport for five years
* Operated the Atlantic Airport for 24 years
* Operated Ames Airport for 25 years - Third busiest airport in the state
* Has given over 1125 check rides
* Inducted in the Iowa Aviation Hall of Fame on June 24, 2000
* His logbook shows over 30,000 flight hours

Thirty thousand flight hours represents:
1250 twenty-four hour days or 3 years, 154 days of twenty-four hour days in the cockpit.
More realistically, 3750 eight-hour days behind the stick/wheel or 10 years, 98 days and five hours piloting an airplane eight hours a day.

Hap flew under a bridge, through a hangar and over Germany.

Is Hartley "Hap" Westbrook a hero?
No. He is an eighteen or twenty-year-old doing a job. He just didn't know how to quit.

The
IOWA AVIATION MUSEUM
of Greenfield, Iowa

Proudly Inducts

Hartley A. (Hap) Westbrook

into the
IOWA AVIATION HALL OF FAME

June 24, 2000

This honor is respectfully bestowed upon Iowans who have contributed significantly to aviation. In all aspects of flight, these men and women pioneered and fostered the growth of aviation with their innovative ideas, unyielding dedication and indomitable spirits. This service has resulted in immeasurable benefits for all.

Iowa is proud of you native sons and daughters and expresses sincere appreciation for your work and dedication in the field of aviation.

★ ★ ★ ★ ★

Certificate presented to Hap Westbrook at the Hall of Fame Dinner, Greenfield, Iowa.

POSTLUDE

In approaching this book, many interviews with family members were collected on tape. They included, among others, Hap Westbrook, daughter Diana, son Dick, sister-in-law Ethel (Bowers) Honnold, and Jane Westbrook.

Although Jane's health was not good, on October 10th, 2000, she was kind enough to spend an hour and one-half with the author, and we bounced through the years recalling incidents, some over seventy years ago. Although it was taxing, Jane entered into it with enthusiasm, and sometimes suspicion, "Now, you aren't going to write that, are you?", seriousness and humor.

On November 3rd, 2000, the family gathered in her home to help Jane celebrate her eighty-second birthday. It was a day of friends, birthday cards, cake and candles. About nine o'clock in the evening the family gathered around the kitchen table where so much activity had focused for so many years.

Quietly, Jane reached for her daughter's hand and said, "My heart hurts. Hold my hand." She then slumped to the table as her heart stopped beating.

Interestingly enough, both of Jane's parents had passed away when they were eighty-two.

Jane Bowers Westbrook's funeral took place on Tuesday, November 7th. Loving words were spoken by the Rev. Cindy McCalmont about Jane's dedication, friendship, understanding, compassion, interest in sports, humor, and several humorous foibles were related. The songs chosen for the service reflected Jane in the purest sense. They were "Nearer My God To Thee," "Amazing Grace," and a taped rendition of "We Are The World."

Tuesday, November 7th, was national Election Day, and Jane, true to form, had cast an absentee ballot since she had never missed a vote. On her funeral day her ballot was counted for her Republican State and County friends, and for George W. Bush for President of the United States.

This photo was taken in Muscatine during their week in Letts after the wedding. The future and dreams of young Americans before entering the world conflict could not be better expressed.

ACKNOWLEDGEMENTS

Special credit should be given to Robert Underhill, Professor Emeritus of English and Speech at Iowa State University and former B-17 Bombardier-Navigator, who was kind enough to read a rough manuscript and make experienced observations and suggestions for the book.

Special thanks to Dave Popelka of McMillen Publishing for his experience, talent and organizatioanl skills that guided this book through the publishing process.

And particularly to Ann Andrews Rudi, whose eagle eye has deposited piles of commas around our house, and whose editing ability is irrefragable. She is also my lovely wife.

To the following sources for background and information:

Behind The Wire - Stalag Luft III - South Compound
By Arnold A Wright
Privately published.

Fields of Little America
By Martin W. Bowman
(1977)
Wensum Books (Norwich) Ltd
33 Orford Place, Norwich

A Wartime Log
By Art and Lee Beltrone
Howell Press (1994)
1147 Riverroad Suite 2
Charlottesville VA 22901
(An excellent account of prisoners' logbooks, poems and personal accounts.)

Combine 13
By Clifford Hopewell
First Edition 1990
Merimore Press
3540 Villaverde #146
Dallas TX
(A highly detailed account of being a POW)

The Mighty Eighth
A History of the U. S. 8th Army Air Force
By Roger Freeman
(1970)
Doubleday and Company

Airfields of the Eighth, Then and Now
By Roger A Freeman
(1978)
Battle of Britain Prints International Ltd
3 New Plaistow Road
London E15 3JA England

The Story of Bombers 1914-1945
By Brian Cooper, Illustrated by John Bachelor
1974
Phoebus Publishing Company
Octopus Books Ltd
59 Grosvenor Street
London W1 England

Deadly Sky - The American Combat Airman in WW II
By John McManus
(2000)
Presidio Press Inc
505 B San Marin Drive - Suite 300
Novato CA 94945-1340

A Wartime Log
By Hartley A Westbrook
O-728041

The Fighting 44th Logbook
Vol. 1 No. 8, Vol. 2 No. 2, Vol. 2 No. 4
44th HMG
P. O. Box 58244
Cincinnati OH 45258-8244

44th Bomb Group Veterans Association
Vol 1 Issue 2   Spring 1995
6304 Meadowridge Drive
Santa Rosa CA 95409

Video - Behind the Wire
Allied Airmen in German Captivity in the Second World War
8th Air Force Historical Society
Al Zimmerman, Writer-Producer